*Women's
History
Resources
in the
Delaware
Valley
Area*

*This work is a project of the
Mayor's Commission for Women of the City of Philadelphia,
and was prepared under its sponsorship and direction.*

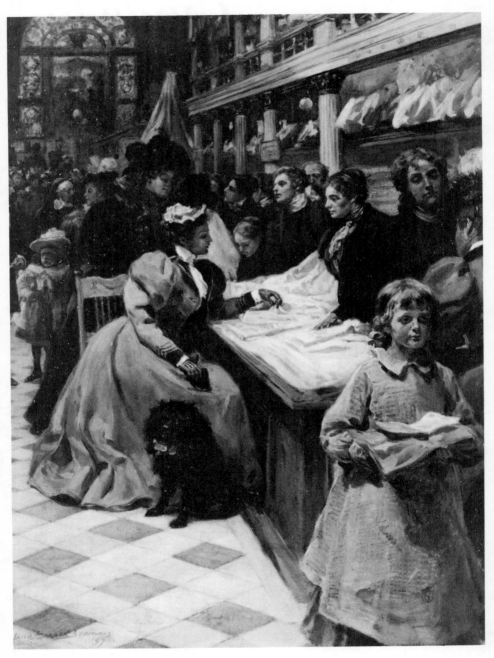

"American Woman in Business" by Alice Barber Stephens, *oil on canvas, 1897
(Collection of the Brandywine River Museum)*

Guide to Women's History Resources in the Delaware Valley Area

edited by
Trina Vaux

with a foreword by
Mary Maples Dunn

The University of Pennsylvania Press

Vaux, Trina.
    Guide to women's history resources in the Delaware
Valley area.

    Bibliography: p.
    Includes index.
    1. Women—Delaware River Valley (N.Y.-Del. and N.J.)
—History—Addresses, essays, lectures. 2. Women—
Pennsylvania—Philadelphia Region—History—Addresses,
essays, lectures. 3. Women—Delaware River Valley (N.Y.-
Del. and N.J.)—History—Bibliography. 4. Women—
Pennsylvania—Philadelphia Region—History—Bibliography.
I. Dunn, Mary Maples. II. Mayor's Commission for Women
of Philadelphia. III. Title.
HQ1438.A118V38   1983   305.4'09749   83-16731
ISBN 0-8122-1168-5 (pbk.)

Printed in the United States of America

Designed by Adrianne Onderdonk Dudden

To women of the future

Who, it is hoped,
will be strengthened by illumination
of the experience of women of the past.

"Friendly Visitor," ca. 1890 (Historical Society of Pennsylvania)

Contents

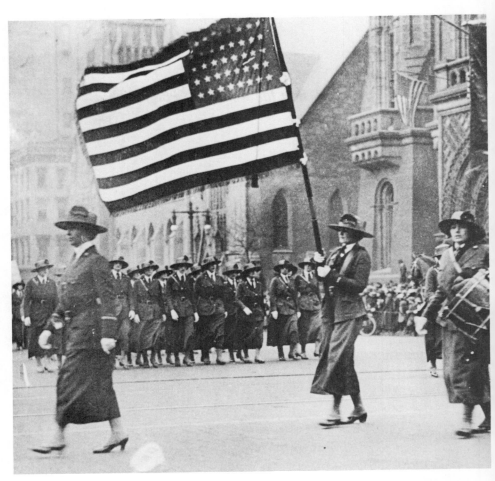

Officers of the Emergency Aid on Parade During World War I (Library Company of Philadelphia)

William J. Green
MAYOR

Diane Kiddy
EXECUTIVE DIRECTOR

The Mayor's Commission for Women is a policy-making and advocacy agency for women within the Mayor's Office of the City of Philadelphia. Its role is to affect city policy so as to improve the status of women within city government and outside it. The Commission serves as a resource and liaison for individuals and organizations in the community, and since its establishment in 1980, has dealt substantively with a large number of pressing issues, and answered the needs of a large number of women. The Commission was established by Mayor William J. Green. Diane Kiddy is its first Executive Director.

Specifically, the Commission makes recommendations for appointments to City boards, commissions, and executive positions. It promotes child care programs, sex equity in education, and women-owned businesses. It also concerns itself with the issues of rape, domestic violence, transit safety, and employment discrimination.

The aim of the Commission's Women's History Project is to bring to public attention the contributions of Philadelphia women, past and present, to our society. Its programs are designed to make available to the city's existing cultural and educational institutions and its community and civic organizations the scholarly resources needed to integrate women's history into their activities.

Women's History Project Oversight Committee

Margaret Hope Bacon
Ernesta Drinker Ballard
Joel Bloom
Barbara Daniel Cox
Mary Maples Dunn
Julia Ericksen
Beverly Harper

Alma Jacobs
Cynthia J. Little
Gordon Marshall
Patricia Owens
Peter Parker
Carroll Smith-Rosenberg
Letty Thall

Mayor's Commission for Women

Marjorie Adler
Carmen Angles
Sister Matthew Anita
Bertha Brown
Dorothy Brown
Priscilla Chialastri
Mary V. Cochran
Amanda L. Coleman
Rosemary O. Davis
Marta Luz Diaz
Sister Falaka Fattah
Helen F. Faust
Rosemarie B. Greco
Anne Hearn
Lillian Holliday
Ruth K. Horwitz
Motria Kushnir
Lynn A. Marks

Barbara W. Mather
Lynne McMahon
Julia Moore Mitchell
Cary Nicholas
Mary Perot Nichols
Patricia Owens
Eloise Owens Strothers
Dianne Semingson
Melonease Shaw-Taylor
Marion B. Tasco
Letty Thall
Patricia Voigt
Reverend Repsie Warren
Paula Weiss
Ruth Smith Wells
Alethia Winston
Cecilia Yep
Martha Zazyczny

Acknowledgments

The Guide to Women's History Resources is the result of much work by many people, most of whom cannot be listed here individually. They range from anonymous archivists who painstakingly filled out questionnaires to reference librarians able to find an obscure dissertation.

The compilation of the book was directed by the Mayor's Commission for Women of the City of Philadelphia, its Executive Director, Diane Kiddy, and its Women's History Oversight Committee as part of a comprehensive two-year women's history project. Funds from PSFS, the Atlantic Richfield Foundation, the Century IV Committee, and the City of Philadelphia made the work possible. The University of Pennsylvania Press, its Associate Director, Malcolm Call, and Ingalill Hjelm, Managing Editor, and other staff members made publication possible in record time.

Each section had its own coterie of unpaid helpers. Each of the institutions listed helped by filling out an intimidating questionnaire and by responding to further queries and general dunning. Staff members of the Bryn Mawr College Archives, the Haverford College Quaker Collection, the Swarthmore College Peace Collection and Friends Historical Library, and the Special Collections of the University of Pennsylvania Van Pelt Library all reacted generously to continual questions on the minutiae of notable women's lives. Barbara McIlvain of the Plastic Club, Shirley Turpin-Parham of the Afro-American Historical and Cultural Museum, Rose McNamara, and Marilyn Hause-Loftus all compiled substantial lists of women, and Dennis Clark, Caroline Golab, Richard Juliani, Barbara Klaczynska, Maxwell Whiteman, and Edwin Wolf provided critical review and suggestions. Zirka Mysko of the Free Library of Philadelphia was miraculously able to check hundreds of bibliographical references. Emilie Gaither and Sara Petrosky assisted with the list of women. Sara Petrosky undertook the awesome task of indexing. Mildred Blithe typed the manuscript with care and accuracy, and Joseph Doyle of the City Duplicating Service was always patient and accommodating with last minute requests.

Staff members of the Historical Society of Pennsylvania and the Library Company of Philadelphia were a constant source of support, suggestions, and information. Linda Stanley and Kenneth Finkel, in particular, eased the task of doing picture research. Rich McMullin of the Office of the City Representative did copy photography of most of the illustrations taken from the Library Company and Historical Society collections.

In the section on notable women numerous entries are quoted directly from *Notable American Women* with the kind permission of Radcliffe College.

I am especially grateful to members of the Oversight Committee who actively assisted in this project: to Margaret Bacon and Ernesta Ballard, whose counsel is always considered and wise; to Mary Dunn, Julia Ericksen, and Carroll Smith-Rosenberg, who somehow found time to review material and make suggestions in the midst of impossible schedules; to Peter Parker, for help with archives and historical societies; to Gordon Marshall, always available to check a reference or advise on any point; and to Cindy Little for her sympathetic ear, critical judgement, and faith.

Finally, my particular thanks go to my husband, Hugh McCauley, for his patience and support, both moral and gastronomic.

In spite of all the assistance given me on this book there are undoubtedly flaws in it. Some I am already aware of, and reasons for them are given elsewhere. Others—institutions missed, notable women ignored, books undiscovered—I will, in accordance with some perverse law, discover only after publication. For sins of omission and commission I apologize; from responsibility for them the persons mentioned above are exempt.

Trina Vaux

Mrs. E. D. Gillespie Receiving Reports from Sub-Committees at the Headquarters of the Women's Centennial Executive Committee. (Frank Leslie's Illustrated Historical Register of the Centennial Exposition 1876)

Foreword

Mary Maples Dunn

The special brilliance of Trina Vaux's approach in the *Guide to Women's History Resources in the Delaware Valley Area* lies in her attempt to be all-inclusive, to cover only our own geographic area, and to utilize an economical research design which relies on librarians', archivists', and curators' new awareness of the importance of the history of women. The appearance of this book is, in itself, testimony to a growing interest on the part of both historians and the general public in the past experience of the women who preceded us here.

Historians recently began to explore the history of women with a new intensity, an intensity which was a product of the women's rights movement. They were initially stymied, however, by the difficulties encountered when they tried to collect evidence. Few women played visible or central public roles. The private papers, even of women from educated and cultivated families, were not so well-regarded and carefully preserved as those of men, unless the women were unusually prominent and noteworthy. Materials that did survive the ravages of time and family, and were placed in public depositories, were hard to find in archival systems organized around famous men or male interests. In libraries and archives catalogue entries under the category "War" invariably exceeded the number under "Women."[*]

But the discovery of individual women was only a small part of the historian's problem. Most of the women who have gone before us were mute—that is, they were born into circumstances in which there was neither the need nor the encouragement (generated in a select few by money, education, or perhaps religion) to leave behind a written record. Those women demand greater ingenuity and skill from the historian, who must learn about them in the aggregate from sources as wide-ranging as jail or hospital records, wills and inventories, club records, church records. And in the past several decades historians have also become more agile and sophisticated in their use of the objects of material culture as historical evidence. Women, after all, spent the greatest part of their lives manipulating their physical surroundings—furnishing and caring for their homes,

[*]*In the* Dewey Decimal Classification and Relative Index *for 1967 (Edition 17) "war" and "wars" were accorded a total of 65 classifications, while "woman," "women," and "women's" totaled 51.*

their families. A great deal can be discovered about a woman's day if you can refurnish her kitchen and her closet and historians learned this art from the archaeologist, art historian, museum curator, and folklorist.

As historians have discovered these needs, librarians and archivists have responded generously. This volume is proof of that. They are now well aware, as this volume will also show, of their resources for the history of women; their catalogues are no longer silent on the subject. Moreover, some bibliographic materials are now available; and it is worth noting that of the dozen bibliographies cited here by Trina Vaux, all but one were published after 1970. Nevertheless, as the Commission for Women discovered, these collections do not have a geographic focus (again, of the dozen bibliographies cited, only one has such a focus), and they tend to include either books or archives, and only rarely the objects of material culture. How, then, could the women of this particular place know where to go to discover their antecedents or investigate the changes that led to their unique, female culture?

It was this last question which prompted this volume, which recovers for us a host of individual women and material from which we can recover thousands more. Who can resist, for example, the household tools of the Mercer Museum, the clothing of the Rebecca Gratz collection in the Museum of American Jewish History, or the abundance of material on Roman Catholic women which is a special revelation of this volume? It is a rich new source in itself, and both the professional and amateur historian will profit from it for years to come.

*Guide to
Women's
History
Resources
in the
Delaware
Valley
Area*

John B. Stetson Co. Sewing Room, ca. 1910 (Division of Archives and Manuscripts, Pennsylvania Historical and Museum Commission, MG219)

Introduction

When the Mayor's Commission for Women was formed in 1980 one of its first tasks was to establish a program that would assure the inclusion of women's history in Philadelphia's 1983 tercentenary celebration. As the Women's History Project developed and gained public recognition, the Commission regularly, and particularly in anticipation of Women's History Week, received queries on women's history from teachers, librarians, women's organizations, and the general public. At that time such requests for information could be answered only haphazardly. We referred people to works of a national scope such as Andrea Hinding's *Women's History Sources*—which covers only archives and leaves out many important local collections; or to *Notable American Women*—where it is difficult to find women of a particular locale and which does not include many women important on a local scale. We sent people to the works of Eugenie Leonard and Sophie Drinker, but they are limited to the colonial and Revolutionary periods; or to the various compilations of notable women of the region, but they are dated.

As we fumbled to answer questions we found that resources on the history of women of the area certainly existed, but were often obscure. Clearly a guide to the region was needed to help make the material more accessible to researchers. Thus was born the *Guide to Women's History Resources in the Delaware Valley Area*. It was to be many things to many people. It was to be useful to the nonspecialist, to the person starting to work in women's history, and to the scholar in another field seeking points of reference. And it was to help students, teachers, librarians, and the staff of cultural institutions to find topics and sources in women's history.

The purposes of the book are manifold: to uncover the history of women in the Delaware Valley and their contributions to our society; to uncover the sources of that history; to encourage archivists to find ways of making the sources more accessible; and to inspire scholars and researchers to investigate and interpret some of the many topics suggested by the available materials.

The scale of the project has from the outset been restricted by limitations of finances, time, and staffing. With one staff member, albeit assisted by generous volunteers, we could not afford the luxury of primary research. We certainly could not cover the material in as much detail as Hinding or

Notable American Women—nor was it desirable to reinvent their wheels. What we did, using those works as a basis, was to establish a more flexible scope, to include museums, corporations, and women's organizations among the institutions, and women of regional as well as national importance among the notables. We also compiled a small bibliography highlighting books and articles dealing specifically with the region.

The process of gathering material for the book was conventional. We set geographical boundaries to cover a historically cohesive area with as many repositories as possible within a reasonable distance: Philadelphia and contiguous Pennsylvania counties, New Jersey north to New Brunswick, Delaware south to Dover. We sent a detailed questionnaire to some 300 archives, museums, libraries, religious congregations, and women's organizations; we culled biographical works; we consulted scholars. (For a reprint of the questionnaire and a list of nonrespondents see Appendix 1 and 2.) Although the last thing any archivist wants to see is yet another questionnaire, institutions and individuals alike responded generously and enthusiastically. This is a subject clearly close to many curatorial and scholarly hearts. And in revealing their hearts these worthy informants answered two important questions: Is there a women's history in the Delaware Valley? Is it retrievable?

The answer to both those questions is an emphatic "Yes—but," as I hope this volume shows. The history exists, but it has yet to be written; it is retrievable, but with difficulty.

Most of the recent work in women's history has been on a very general, national scale or on a very small scale. There are histories of women in America, collections of documents that illustrate the developing self-awareness of women, and works on the experience of women of a particular period. Conversely, journal articles single out one diary or activity; theses may cover a broader scope but in a very specific area. The work done by Sophie Drinker, Eugenie Leonard, and others in the 1940s and 1950s is invaluable on the eighteenth century, but nothing like it has been done on the nineteenth or early twentieth centuries.

While we lament the lack of a complete picture of women in Delaware Valley history, the problems of painting it are clear and are reflected in the present work. The difficulty with women in history is that their life does not conform to traditional patterns of research. Women do not answer to questions that have to do with the rise and fall of nations and power structures because, with some exceptions, they carry out their activities apart from the established centers of power. Often their influence is felt in different ways from that of men. Likewise, the records of their life tend not to be found in the main catalogues of libraries and archives.

Women's history sources are often hidden because cataloguers have not used women as a category, although some are now beginning to do so. Much valuable material is included in record groups or in general topical series or family papers under men's names, but considerable effort is required to root it out. (Andrea Hinding's *Women's History Sources* is helpful in describing such material in major archives.)

Although somewhat hidden, white middle-class women of the majority Protestant culture are comparatively well represented in major institutions, either through individual women, families, or organizations. Immigrants, blacks, and laboring women are much more obscure. In some cases the burdens of a basic existence—child rearing, making a living—do not afford opportunities for a more public contribution to society. Survival is notable enough. When women do move outside the home they usually do so within their own ethnic communities, which are not as well documented as the "mainstream" culture. Such women tend not to be represented in large general repositories but in smaller, more specific, or newer archives. The various Roman Catholic religious congregations, for instance, hold much valuable material on women whose only opportunity to achieve notability beyond the home was to join the church.

The reasons for the obscurity of women's history sources naturally lead to the history itself. This book does not purport to give a complete history of women in the Delaware Valley; a great deal more research is necessary before that can be done. Some conclusions can be drawn, however, based on the materials in this Guide. What follows is an overview, of necessity, general, of the themes and the women that have put the Delaware Valley in the vanguard of women's history.

Armegott Printz (American Swedish
Historical Foundation and Museum)

Hannah Callowhill Penn (Historical
Society of Pennsylvania)

Delaware Valley Women's History: An Overview

Three women stand out from the very beginning of settlement in the Delaware Valley: Armegott Printz Papegoja in New Sweden, Hannah Penn in Pennsylvania, and Elizabeth Haddon Estaugh in New Jersey. Armegott Printz managed her father's colony. Hannah Penn was her husband's executrix and acting Proprietor from the time of his incapacitating stroke in 1712, and Elizabeth Haddon managed her own estates and founded Haddonfield in New Jersey.

A set of particular circumstances of law, geography, training, and family conspired to give these three women more power than any woman has ever since exercised in this region. It should be noted that two of them were Quakers, members of a dissenting faith that regarded women as men's equals under God and that had a particular concern for the education of girls as well as boys. The Quaker attitude toward women exerted a beneficial influence on the position of members of the sex in the Delaware Valley. Certainly, in terms of numbers, Quakers are heavily represented among notable women of the area throughout the seventeenth, eighteenth, and nineteenth centuries. Many of them, in addition to other achievements, were "Public Friends" who traveled throughout this country and England visiting Quaker Meetings and spreading the light. Others, anonymous wives of Public Friends, took on heavy responsibilities during the prolonged absences of their husbands.

In the seventeenth and eighteenth centuries women's activities were in some ways less circumscribed and were granted more recognition than they were in the nineteenth century. For the colonial family in a pre-industrial society, sharing of the tasks of daily living was essential and acknowledgement was, at least in theory, afforded to all who contributed to the general well being. Certainly, there was plenty of "housework," but the household economy included enterprises such as farming, commerce, and manufacture, which gave women a large scope.

On the other hand, in legal terms, a married woman had very few rights except to support by her husband and the use, but not control, of one-third of his estate on his death. Unless she had arranged an ante-nuptial agreement to the contrary, her husband had complete control of her property and of everything we might today consider to be held in common. Single women and widows, without the protection of a husband, were protected by law. They could conduct business, write contracts, and manage property. But they more often had to marry or remarry to survive. Single and rich in colonial America, a woman could do very well. Others had to rely on beneficence and business acumen in their husbands.

Women could not rely on education in the colonial period. Upper-class girls whose brothers had tutors might share lessons; some went to unprofessional Dame Schools; others learned somehow to read and write from busy parents or older siblings. In 1754 Anthony Benezet founded a school unique in its high standards that accepted girls. But in general education for girls was haphazard at best, and only available to those of means. Certainly, females did not pass through the doors of the College, Academy, and Charitable School (later to become the University of Pennsylvania) when it was chartered in 1755.

Nevertheless, with or without husbands, and with or without education, women were active in a wide range of occupations. They engaged in commerce, like Margaret Duncan, also a philanthropist, or Betsy Ross, who would not have been asked to make the flag had she not had a thriving upholstery business. Many women were printers, such as Mary Katherine Goddard, also a postmaster, who was commissioned by Congress to print the first official Declaration of Independence distributed to state legislatures. Anna Nutt owned iron foundries. Sybilla Masters invented a machine for grinding corn and sold the ground meal as "Tuscarora Rice," advertised as a cure for consumption. Although the patent was issued in her husband's name and the potion was not unlike hominy, Sybilla may have been the nation's first woman inventor as well as its first purveyor of patent medicine.

In Philadelphia, the second largest English-speaking city in the world, women actively participated in a lively social and intellectual life. Elizabeth Drinker, diarist, and Elizabeth Graeme Ferguson, litterateur and poet, are among the best known, but there are others. Susannah Wright, although somewhat isolated on the frontier, nevertheless took part in a larger world through writing poetry, contributing to magazines, and corresponding with the leading intellectuals of the day. Patience Wright of New Jersey was acclaimed in London for her wax sculptures, which, it is thought, she used to conceal messages useful to the Revolutionary cause.

But there is a trap here. These are the women about whom we know because they happen to have left records. They become the "great white women" of history simply because they lived in comfortable circumstances and had the time to write letters and diaries or left examples of their work. They owned property, had married well, or had a means of making a living. They were also educated. (Elizabeth Drinker attended Anthony Benezet's school.) The picture was not so rosy for those less well situated: servants, wives and daughters of poor men, and the majority of black women. The tasks of the colonial housewife without help were many and arduous. For some, their own domestic chores were multiplied by the need to take on those of others in order to increase the family income. Indentured servants and slaves often had the added burden of living away from their family, trapped in a household which might or might not be benevolent. In an age when social welfare programs relied on haphazard individual philanthropy, the poorhouse was a constant reality (although the Quakers provided more help than was available in other places). For slaves, the presence and support of a free black community offered some small hope. But for women, black and white alike, whose education was determined by parental status and whim and whose activity was constrained by notions of morality, upward mobility was severely limited.

The Revolutionary War was a turning point for the nation; it was also a turning point for American women. In general, women were politicized by the experience. They took sides and participated in the ideological ferment of the time. Some, like the many Molly Pitchers, were heroic in the traditional sense; many others took on larger responsibilities in the absence of their husbands. Working women gained employment in war production. The Philadelphia Ladies Association, headed by Esther de Berdt Reed, and a similar organization in New Jersey, engaged in war relief work, raising money and sewing shirts for Washington's army. Some women were occasional spies, such as Lydia Darragh, who was also a nurse, midwife, and undertaker.

Although the success of the Revolution was a general triumph, it may not have had such a liberating effect on women. Wives had to give up their managerial role on the return of their conquering hero-husbands. The latitude of a free-wheeling colonial society tightened as a new nation got down to the serious business of governing itself. And in spite of Abigail Adams's instructions to her husband to "Remember the Ladies," there was nothing in the Constitution to give women particular cause to rejoice. (In New Jersey a 1790 law gave women the right to vote, but it was repealed in 1807.) The men who launched and guided the first steps of the Republic, intent on emulating a patriarchal Roman model, had little concern for remembering ladies—unless it was in the privacy of their home. (Certainly, those women in any period who are close to power may affect the wielding of it. Philadelphia's own Roman matron, Dolley Madison, apparently did not do so directly, although she socially enlivened both Philadelphia and Washington.)

In the nineteenth century middle- and upper-class women retreated to the home and to "ladylike" tasks—good works, education, writing, art. The retreat was reinforced by industrialization, the movement of commerce away from the home, and the notion of the idle wife as status symbol for a successful male who could earn enough to support a family unassisted. In 1847 Sarah Josepha Buell Hale, from her editor's desk at *Godey's Lady's Book* wrote: "We are true to the creed that the civilization of the world is to be the work of woman . . ."[1] (Mrs. Hale, whose opinions were widely read, was a staunch advocate of women's influence and responsibilities, but not of women's rights.) Women were to be the keepers of the cultural flames of religion and morality; they were to guard the temples of the cult of domesticity. Although this role may not have been as large a one as the female veterans of the Revolution might have liked, at least it was recognized as valuable. The importance assigned to the home, the temple of the Republic, legitimized women's traditional tasks.

Now that they had a defined role, women needed proper schooling in order to be better wives and mothers. Amid much discussion of the nature of an education appropriate to the keepers of the nation's culture, Benjamin Rush and others founded the Philadelphia Young Ladies Academy in 1787. In 1799 the Quakers established Westtown, a coeducational boarding school. They also ran the Clarkson School for blacks. The women who attended these new academies gained a profession suitable to the nurturing sex—teaching—which in turn provided competent staff for charity schools, such as the one founded in 1796 by the Society for the Free Instruction of Female Children (a Quaker women's organization).

As the nineteenth century advanced, women's need for greater educational opportunities increased. Some few schools were coeducational. The Pennsylvania Academy of the Fine Arts accepted women in "separate but equal" classes and as early as 1824 Sarah and Anna Peale were on the Academy's Board of Academicians. In addition, the Philadelphia area spawned impressive institutions of higher learning expressly for women. In 1844 Sarah Worthington King Peter, with the assistance of the Franklin Institute, established the Philadelphia School of Design for Women (now Moore College of Art). Mrs. Peter's aim was to provide American women with training in practical design for Philadelphia's thriving textile, wallpaper, bookmaking, and other industries. Her school, which had started in her house, expanded, thrived, and maintained a high standing in the fine as well as industrial and commercial arts. Emily Sartain was its director from 1886 to 1919, and many notable female as well as male artists taught there, Alice Barber Stephens among them.

Philadelphia's other major women's educational institution dating from the pre–Civil War period was the Female Medical College of Pennsylvania (now the Medical College of Pennsylvania), founded by a group of Quakers in 1850. Although many women in the colonial period had practiced medicine, the professionalization of the healing arts increasingly limited the field to men; women were excluded from the new training schools and from practicing in hospitals. The Female Medical College afforded them the training denied elsewhere, and was a national mecca for aspiring women doctors. Its roster of graduates is a "who's who" of nineteenth-century women in medicine and medical missionaries. Ann Preston, in the first graduating class, was the first woman dean, and established the Women's Hospital in 1861 to offer clinical training to the College's students. Hannah Myers Longshore, also in the first class, taught, had her own practice, and gave public lectures on medical topics. Anna Broomall, obstetrician and medical educator, was also a graduate.

Once out of the Medical College, these early "doctoresses" had a difficult career ahead. Police guarded their 1851 commencement exercises to prevent violence threatened by male medical students, and women were not admitted to the Philadelphia County Medical Society until 1888.

Presumably, the graduates of a two-year normal school for girls, established in 1848, had an easier time in a profession in which women were accepted. By 1851 there were 699 women teaching in the Philadelphia public schools, albeit at lower pay than the 82 men.

In the first half of the nineteenth century women in the Delaware Valley, like women throughout the country, were assigned a role and an area of influence. But within their prescribed sphere they tended to more than their knitting. Some were pioneers in education, medicine, and art. Others carried out Sarah Hale's injunction to civilize the world through social reform. The latter efforts can be viewed as another extension of domestic morality to the public sphere, yet their importance is immense in the areas of political ideology as well as practical social welfare.

Much work, heavily influenced by the Quakers, focused on the abolition of slavery. The activity of Lucretia Mott, Mary Grew, the Grimké sisters, and the Philadelphia Female Anti-Slavery Society, founded in 1833, became intertwined, by the 1840s, in the women's rights movement. Quaker women abolitionists, accustomed to speak in meeting, considered it natural to lecture in public to "promiscuous" (sexually mixed) audiences. Unfortunately, the public did not always share that view, and the women abolitionists were constantly barraged with verbal abuse, volleys of vegetation, and real violence. In 1838, the night after Abby Kelley (later Foster) spoke at the second women's anti-slavery convention in Pennsylvania Hall, the new building, erected expressly for abolition meetings, was burned to the ground. (It should be noted that Quakers were divided on the subjects of women's rights and abolitionism. The Hicksite branch, of which Lucretia Mott was a member, was more active in these areas than was the Orthodox.)

The experience of Lucretia Mott, Mary Grew, Sarah Pugh, and others at the World Anti-Slavery Convention in London in 1840 should by now be a familiar tale. The fact that they were relegated to the status of silent observers from the gallery, and were not accepted as delegates on account of their sex, persuaded them to fight for women's rights as well as those of blacks. It also persuaded one young observer, Elizabeth Cady Stanton (who had accompanied her delegate husband to London) to do the same, and led to the Seneca Falls Convention of 1848.

Of course, the champions of the abolitionist cause were not all white. The Philadelphia Female Anti-Slavery Society is a rare example of an organization in which black and white women worked very closely together. Sarah Mapps Douglass, Harriet Forten Purvis, and Hester Reckless were active in the Society. Many of them also worked on the Underground Railroad, along with Sarah Bass Allen and others. Mary Ann Shadd Cary, born in Wilmington, moved to Windsor, Ontario, to minister to the refugee community there. Her newspaper, the "Provincial Freeman," proclaimed her "the first colored woman on the American continent to establish and edit a weekly newspaper."[2]

The abolitionists knew that education was an important factor in the liberation of black people. In the eighteenth and early nineteenth centuries the Quakers had founded schools for blacks. In 1837 they established another which by 1852 had become the Institute for Colored Youth (now

Cheyney State College). This school, offering intellectual and manual training, was the springboard for many black women. Sarah Douglass administered the primary girls department in its early period. Later Fanny Marion Jackson Coppin, principal for over thirty years, initiated normal school training in 1871 and industrial skills in 1889.

After 1861 a number of Delaware Valley women participated in another education enterprise, the Port Royal Experiment. Charlotte Forten Grimké and Martha Schofield both taught in the schools for newly freed blacks on the Sea Islands of South Carolina. Cornelia Hancock, after distinguished service as a nurse at Gettysburg, Washington, and City Point, Virginia, established what became the Laing School for black children in Charleston. The school was supported in large part by Hancock's Delaware Valley Quaker friends.

Active as they were, Quakers did not have a monopoly on good works. Upper-class women of all denominations ministered to the poor through the Female Association for the Relief of Women and Children in Reduced Circumstances; they pressed for Indian rights and prison reform. Catholic women founded the Rosine Association in 1847 "To rescue from vice and degradation a class of women who have forfeited their claim to the respect of the virtuous."[3] The Association established a house for wayward women and its members regularly made "friendly visits" to brothels.

During the nineteenth century a number of Roman Catholic orders took root in Philadelphia. Initially instituted as missions to the new land, religious congregations afforded an opportunity for women to play an active intellectual and service role within the bounds of respectability. They also were a great educational force, at first instilling European values and culture to upper-class girls, later providing learning at low cost for immigrant groups.

The Sisters of the Holy Child Jesus, established in Philadelphia in 1846, was founded by Cornelia Connelly, a convert whose religious work was carried out in spite of harrassment by her erratic former husband. Much later, in 1891, another local woman, Mother Mary Katharine Drexel, gave herself and her fortune to the establishment of the Sisters of the Blessed Sacrament for Indians and Colored Peoples. (Her sisters, Elizabeth Drexel Smith and Louise Bouvier Drexel Morrell, also gave generously to the betterment of blacks and Indians). Other orders had sprung up in the intervening years: the Sisters of St. Joseph in 1847 and of St. Francis in 1855, followed by the Sisters of the Immaculate Heart of Mary in 1858. The Sisters of St. Basil, although the earliest Catholic order in the world (dating from the fourth century), did not appear here until 1911 to minister to newly-arrived Ukrainian immigrants.

While Sarah Bass Allen may have had considerable influence on the running of Mother Bethel Church and Anna Howard Shaw was the first woman ordained as a Methodist minister, most non-Quaker Protestant women carried out church work at the lay level. As early as 1800 church women participated in charitable activities such as the Magdalen Society, a Protestant counterpart to the Rosine Association. They also became missionaries in this country and abroad. In the Jewish community, Rebecca Gratz did more than exercise her beauty and sit for her portrait in *Ivanhoe;* in 1838 she founded the Hebrew Sunday School Society for Jewish boys and girls and was involved throughout her life in a host of charitable causes, both Jewish and non-sectarian. The Rebecca Gratz Club, founded in 1904 to assist Jewish immigrant women, was named for her, and still exists as a non-sectarian rehabilitation center for teenage girls.

The industrial expansion of the nineteenth century affected the lives of rich and poor women alike. For those who could afford servants it meant extra time to engage in charitable and reform activities. A very few, like Rebecca Lukens, with her iron mills, engaged directly in nineteenth-century progress and reaped its full benefits. For working women industrialization meant toiling in the sweat shops of the garment trade for a pittance. In the 1840s weekly wages for a woman laborer in a match factory were between $2.50 and $3.00. Men could find some hope in the beginnings of a union movement; women could not. In 1869 the National Labor Union convening in Philadelphia would not recognize Susan B. Anthony as a delegate from the Workingwomen's Protective Association.

For black working women the situation was worse. They were excluded from the garment trade. They faced stiff competition in the area of domestic service from middle- and late-century immigrants. Before the Civil War a servant might receive $1.00 per week plus board.

Some black women nevertheless did succeed: Henrietta Bowers Duterte made enough money as an undertaker to be a philanthropist as well; Frances Harper was a noted poet and author as well as lecturer and reformer; and many taught, including Rebecca Cole, also a physician and the first black graduate of the Female Medical College.

The Civil War was a proving ground for women and their organizational abilities; the experience they gained in the war effort gave them professional status in a number of fields. Nursing and hospital administration were of necessity open to all, and women such as Abigail Gibbons, Mary Holstein, and Cornelia Hancock rendered distinguished service. Many Philadelphians, including Elizabeth Duane Gillespie, organized the great Sanitary Fair, which in a single day on Logan Square in 1864 raised a million dollars for war relief.

The experience of the nurses and the recognition of their capabilities certainly influenced the development of nursing and enabled later women such as Linda Richards to make of it a real profession. Likewise, the ladies of the Sanitary Commission gained such a reputation in that enterprise that they were asked to assist in fund raising for the 1876 Centennial Exposition. Under the direction of Mrs. Gillespie, the Women's Centennial Committee was a highly organized machine. After raising over $40,000 for the celebration at large, they raised another $30,000 for the Women's Pavilion—the first at any exposition—and proceeded to fill it with exhibits, events, and a model kindergarten. From it they published a newspaper, "The New Century for Women," entirely written and printed by women. (Mrs. Gillespie later regretted that the building itself was designed by Hermann Joseph

Schwartzmann and not by a woman. A local female architect would certainly have been hard to find; Minerva Parker Nichols, later to be a successful practitioner, was only fifteen at the time.)

The celebration of the centennial of the Declaration of Independence presented an obvious opportunity for the more politically active—the women's rights advocates—to state their case. Susan B. Anthony's unauthorized July 4th reading of the Women's Declaration of Independence to a rather surprised audience at Independence Hall is well known.

Although there is a distinction between the political reformers, the suffragists (descended from the abolitionists) and the charity workers and organizers, most of the women mentioned here for their other achievements were women's rights advocates to a greater or lesser degree. And the Delaware Valley had its share of radical suffragists. In 1868 a group of Vineland women attempted to vote in the presidential election. In 1871 Carrie Burnham Kilgore, a teacher and lawyer, attempted to vote in Philadelphia. She argued her own case before the State Supreme Court—and lost.

Women had been active in charity and social welfare before the war; they were even more so after it. And they were pioneers in developing these crusades into the modern field of social work. Although the Quakers had long ago ceased to be predominant in numbers or power, their reform spirit was certainly still alive. "Friendly visitors" kept watch over the city's poor neighborhoods, ministering particularly to women and children. Hannah Fox and Helen Parrish bought, renovated, and rented houses at low rates to workers and their families. Susan Wharton started the St. Mary's Street Library in 1884 (five years before Jane Addams moved to Hull House in Chicago), which quickly became a full settlement operation offering classes, banking assistance, and medical help. In 1896 the Octavia Hill Association was established by members of the Civic Club. It provided reasonable housing and also lobbied for housing legislation. Cornelia Hancock and Edith Wright developed a similar housing project called Wrightstown in South Philadelphia. And Hancock was also instrumental in the founding of the Children's Aid and Family Service Societies.

Other women promoted temperance and peace. Mary Bonney and Amelia Quinton worked for Indian rights, Caroline Hollingsworth Pemberton and others worked for rights for black people. Emma and Mary Garrett invented new methods for teaching the deaf. Emily Perkins Bissell, a Delaware anti-suffragist, initiated the Christmas Seal to raise funds for tuberculosis research. Upper- and middle-class women such as Ella Bloor, Helen Marot, and Florence Kelley fought for labor reform.

In the post–Civil War period, while women sought to improve the lot of others, they also sought to improve themselves. They fostered educational opportunities on a broader scale. Miss Irwin opened her doors to students in 1869. The Quakers established coeducational Swarthmore College in 1871. Bryn Mawr College was founded in 1885 by a Quaker, and shortly thereafter the Misses Shipley, also Quakers, established a preparatory school for the college.

M. Carey Thomas, feminist, the molder and second president of Bryn Mawr (the first president, according to usual practice, was a man), was determined to provide women with an education comparable to that available to men at the venerable universities. Under her direction the college did just that, and like the Female Medical College in its sphere, educated and hired as faculty many distinguished women. (A list that included all the notable women who were educated at Bryn Mawr and the Female Medical College, regardless of where they came from or went afterwards, would be twice as long as the one in this volume.) The fact that these two institutions continued to flourish, even after the larger medical schools and universities opened their doors to women, is evidence of their quality.

Other local leaders in education were Laura Horner Carnell, influential in the early development of Temple University, and Anna Hallowell, active in the kindergarten movement, who in 1886 became the first female member of the Philadelphia Board of Education. Anna Beach Pratt, as director of the White-Williams Foundation for Girls (formerly the Magdalen Society) was a pioneer in vocational guidance for students. Martha Falconer turned the House of Refuge into a model—the Sleighton School—and with others organized the Philadelphia Training School for Social Work.

During the first half of the twentieth century the Roman Catholic orders expanded their educational range with Chestnut Hill, Holy Family, and Rosemont Colleges, among others. In 1918 Mabel Smith Douglass established the New Jersey College for Women with the help of the New Jersey women's clubs, and under the charter of Rutgers University. It was later renamed Douglass College in her honor.

Women's drive for self-improvement also gave rise to the club movement in the last half of the nineteenth century. The organizations they founded not only offered opportunities for "networking," as we would call it, and conviviality, but also continuing education. The most elite was the Acorn Club, established in 1889, of which Sara Yorke Stevenson, archaeologist and a member of the American Philosophical Society, was president for twenty-five years. In 1877 Eliza Sproat Turner and others founded the New Century Club to provide women "a forum for the discussion of their interests." By 1882 it had given birth to the New Century Guild which offered practical courses for working women. Florence Kelley, social reformer and Secretary of the National Consumer's League, taught here, as did Martha Falconer, as well as the grande dame of the Victorian kitchen and purveyor of opinionated household hints, Sarah Tyson Rorer. The activities of the Guild led in turn, and with the help of Anthony J. Drexel, to the establishment in 1891 of Drexel University, which offered technical training to both sexes.

Women in Delaware joined the New Century Club of Wilmington, and in New Jersey they were members of the Women's Club of Camden. The YWCA and YWHA were part of the same movement, as were the numerous patriotic societies in which women were involved. The American Association of University Women was established by graduates of institutions of higher learning recently opened to females.

Most of the women's clubs were segregated. The solidarity of the abolitionist movement had been lost after the Civil War, and for the most part black and white women had gone separate ways. Before the war black women of means established the Minerva and Edgeworth Literary Associations. After the war their club work concentrated on charitable activities and racial uplift.

Throughout the nineteenth century the number of professions open to women was small. Women doctors had limited opportunities in private practice and many turned to education or opened public clinics. Others, like Anna Kugler, became missionaries. Lawyers were rare. Carrie Kilgore was an active suffragist as well as the first woman graduate of the University of Pennsylvania Law School in 1883. In the same year Mary Ann Shadd Cary received her degree from the Howard University Law School, but apparently was never admitted to the bar.

Scientists were more plentiful. Graceanna Lewis, a teacher, temperance worker, and abolitionist, member of the Academy of Natural Sciences and American Philosophical Society, is noted for her work in ornithology. Adele Fielde, a missionary and suffragist, was also an entomologist. Mary Adelia Treat, a perceptive observer of the natural phenomena of the Pine Barrens, assisted Darwin by mail from her home in Vineland, New Jersey. Later, Mary Vaux Walcott's watercolors documenting wildflowers gave her scientific status.

The theatre, because of its easygoing atmosphere, was always considered suspect by moralists. For middle-class women a theatrical career meant the end of respectability. And this must have been especially true in a Delaware Valley still influenced by conservative Quaker tradition. Nevertheless, the great Drew/Barrymore clan flourished here, and Fanny Kemble railed against slavery when she was not treading the boards. But it was Charlotte Cushman, herself a paragon of respectability, an actress, and manager of the Walnut Street Theatre, who helped to mitigate the prejudice against female thespians. (In 1907 a group of Philadelphia ladies founded a haven for actresses, named the Charlotte Cushman Club in her honor.) At the mid-nineteenth century Mary Ann Lee, as the first American to dance "Giselle," was proving that Europe had no monopoly on dance technique.

The world of professional music was difficult for an American woman to join, but two patrons stand out: Mary Louise Curtis Bok Zimbalist founded the Curtis Institute of Music and was involved in the Settlement Music School; Frances Wister invented and for many years directed the Women's Committees of the Philadelphia Orchestra. Lucy McKim Garrison collected and published slave songs. Elizabeth Taylor Greenfield, a singer, gained renown as the "Black Swan," as did Bessie Smith for her Blues. Jeanette MacDonald was a native daughter as well.

The two areas in which women flourished were writing and art. Nathaniel Hawthorne jealously railed against the "damned mob of scribbling women" whose works sold better than his. Susannah Haswell Rowson, an actress and playwright as well as a novelist, was undoubtedly the most popular of the "mob." Her *Charlotte Temple* went through forty editions in her own lifetime and many more thereafter. Writing was a socially acceptable means of support and also an economic necessity for later women such as Rebecca Harding Davis. Agnes Repplier achieved national renown as an essayist. Many black women were writers and journalists as well, including Sarah Mapps Douglass, Charlotte Forten Grimké, and Frances Harper. Harper's "The Two Offers" is thought to be the first short story published by a black American.

The editors of the two most popular in a large field of magazines for women—Sarah Hale of *Godey's Lady's Book* and later Louisa Knapp Curtis of the *Ladies Home Journal*—not only earned a living for themselves, but also provided a forum and an income for other women writers and greatly influenced the female population of the entire country. In 1860 Godey's boasted as many as a million readers whom it plied with poems, stories, and advice on everything from morality to needlepoint.

Art—an extension of traditional accomplishments—was another field open to women. The three Peale sisters obviously took advantage of their heritage. Many nineteenth-century women became illustrators—Emily Sartain, a painter and engraver, and Alice Barber Stephens of the Howard Pyle School are but two examples. The Plastic Club, an art club for women established in 1897, had a large and active membership. Cecilia Beaux and especially Mary Cassatt are important figures on a national and international scale. Cecilia Beaux was a member of the Plastic Club and New Century Club, and in 1895 was the first woman to teach at the Pennsylvania Academy of the Fine Arts. The talents of Susan MacDowell Eakins have unfortunately been overshadowed by those of her husband. Meta Fuller, a black woman, gained some renown in Paris for her sculpture. Violet Oakley executed murals commissioned by both public authorities and private individuals.

The women of the Delaware Valley began the nineteenth century, as did their sisters throughout the country, with an assigned domestic role. What they did with that role was extraordinary. They carried out Sarah Hale's directive to take on "the civilization of the world" at home, on the frontier, and abroad. In doing so, by the turn of the twentieth century they had professionalized their traditional tasks: education, social welfare, caring for the sick, philanthropic organization. They also had made large contributions to art and literature.

Charlotte Amanda Brown, a physician from the Delaware Valley, founded San Francisco Children's Hospital. Alice Bennett was also a hospital superintendent. Anna Broomall was a foremost obstetrician, and Catharine MacFarlane founded a cancer detection clinic. All are twentieth-century examples of the followers of Ann Preston.

In this century the daughters of Friendly Visitors might be social workers trained at the Bryn Mawr Graduate School of Social Work and Social Research; the spiritual descendants of Cornelia Hancock might be graduates of the School of Nursing at the Hospital of the University of Pennsylvania; the new teachers might have received their credentials at Cheyney or West Chester.

Other fields in which women gained professional status, such as anthropology and psychology, were new enough not to have acquired formalized sexual barriers. Louise Bush-Brown directed the Pennsylvania School of Horticulture for Women and founded the Neighborhood Garden Association. The influence on classical archaeology of Bryn Mawr College's Mary Hamilton Swindler was prodigious. Other Bryn Mawr professors did distinguished work in literature and the sciences.

Nevertheless, it was not until 1920 that women were enfranchised, through the efforts of Alice Paul and many others. Much hard work by the likes of Mary Foley Grossman and Dorothy Bellanca was necessary to improve the working woman's situation.

Many of the leading women of any time are, of course, persons of means who can afford household help. Others remain single and thus avoid some domestic toil. But many of the women mentioned here had children to raise, a family to care for. (In most cases the latter did not become publicly active until after their children had grown.) For the working woman who every day left a grueling factory job to return home to an equally grueling household job, or who toiled a double day with piecework, there was little time for other pursuits except perhaps those which might better her lot. The lucky ones might in the 1920s and 1930s attend the Bryn Mawr Summer School for Women Workers in Industry; a typist or department store clerk might take evening courses at Drexel.

Women with free time continued to be active in clubs and charitable work. Newly arrived immigrants participated in church organizations and the women's versions of fraternal societies such as the Union of Polish Women. Jewish women established Hadassah and B'nai B'rith chapters. Black women organized the National Association for Colored Women and a number of sororities supporting charitable causes.

During the first and second world wars many women worked at home and abroad in war relief, most notably Julia Branson and Emma Cadbury of the American Friends Service Committee, and Caroline Moore and Bertha Coles. Others were pacifists, like Hannah Clothier Hull and Mabel Vernon, both of whom were pillars of the Women's International League for Peace and Freedom.

After the passage of the Nineteenth Amendment in 1920 agitation for women's rights lessened considerably. Alice Paul in 1923 began the battle for the Equal Rights Amendment (or Lucretia Mott Amendment as she called it) but with the poor results we have recently seen. The League of Women Voters formed to educate women for full participation in a democratic society. Nevertheless, politics and influential government work were areas still virtually closed to women. Frances Perkins, Roosevelt's Secretary of Labor, and Crystal Dreda Byrd Fauset, the first black woman state legislator, are exceptions to the rule.

The Delaware Valley, and Philadelphia in particular, has always taken pride in being an area of "firsts." Certainly, this was true in the eighteenth and a large part of the nineteenth centuries, and it is true for women's history no less than for history in general. Most of the women mentioned here were in the vanguard of their fields; they are significant nationally and, in some cases, internationally. Many of the institutions they founded were unique in their time.

It is obvious, even from this limited view, that women of the Delaware Valley have taken a significant role in the development of our society and culture in many ways and in many spheres. The records of their life may be somewhat hidden, but the effort to uncover them will reward the diligent. My hope is that the material presented here will encourage research in areas still untapped. More important, I hope this book will assist in reconstructing the whole story of women so that ultimately they can take their place in a larger history that includes all of us, regardless of ethnic or racial inheritance, sex, and economic position.

Notes

1. *Quoted in Russell F. Weigley, ed.* Philadelphia: A 300 Year History *(New York, 1982), p. 336.*
2. *Quoted in Edward T. James, ed.* Notable American Women: 1607–1950 *(Cambridge, Mass., 1971),* 1:300.
3. *Quoted in* Philadelphia, *pp. 335–36.*

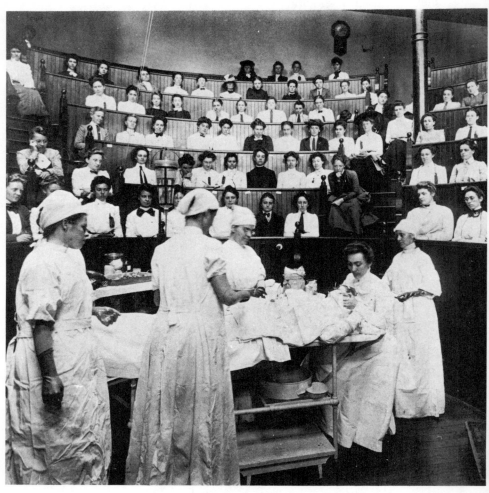

Operating Room/Clinic, Women's Medical College, 1903 (Archives and Special Collections on Women in Medicine, Medical College of Pennsylvania)

Institutions

The following section contains entries for all of the institutions that responded to the Women's History Project questionnaire and that have materials on Delaware Valley women's history unique in quality, massive in quantity, or both. (The questionnaire is reprinted in the Appendix, as is a list of institutions that did not respond or responded negatively.) The geographical area covered is Philadelphia and contiguous Pennsylvania counties, New Jersey north to New Brunswick, and Delaware south to Dover.

In preparing the entries here I have relied entirely on information supplied by the institutions, since resources were not available to make individual inspections and searches through material. Therefore, each entry reflects the interests and current knowledge of a staff archivist or curator. It is hoped that the statements on women's material, taken in the context of the size of collection and areas of interest, will give a clear picture of what each institution holds, regardless of differences in length and detail of the entries.

Accessibility of women's material through finding aids varies widely from one institution to another. Catalogues and guides, like the materials they describe, have been created over a number of years and reflect the interests and professional standards of different staff members. Only recently have efforts been made to catalogue for retrieval of women, and in most institutions the work is far from complete. Individual persons are still much easier to find than general subjects. Nevertheless, it is my hope that the material here will help to guide the researcher a few steps beyond the accessible individuals to other areas of inquiry.

We all owe a debt to Andrea Hinding's massive *Women's History Sources* which gives detailed information on archives and manuscript collections. For institutions listed in that work I have given the entry numbers to aid the reader in further investigation. An asterisk following the number indicates that the Hinding entry is incomplete or otherwise erroneous.

ACADEMY OF NATURAL SCIENCES OF PHILADELPHIA   PPAN

Library, Archive, Museum, Scientific Research Facility
Founded 1812

19th and Race Streets   (215) 299–1040/41
Philadelphia, Pa. 19103   Contact: Manuscript/Archives Librarian

Mon.—Fri. 9:00am—5:00pm   No fee

Published Guides: *Guide to Manuscript Collections in the Academy, Minutes and Correspondence of the Academy.*
Size of Collection: Approx. 190,000 items.
Areas of Interest: Archives of the Academy, 1812 to the present. Materials include the papers of staff and local scientists in natural history, any date; natural history art, photographs relating to the Academy and/or natural history; archives of organizations associated with the Academy (e.g. American Entomological Society, Delaware Valley Ornithological Club).
Women's Material: Includes the papers of Adele Marion Fielde, letters of Graceanna Lewis, watercolor illustrations of Helen Lawson and Helen Winchester, minutes of the Academy's Women's Committee from its inception, 1954 to the present, and the papers of Dr. Ruth Patrick (not yet deposited).

See Hinding 14,875–14,880

ACADEMY OF THE NEW CHURCH—ARCHIVES   PBa

Archive
Founded 1876

2815 Huntingdon Pike   (215) 947–4200 ext. 400
Bryn Athyn, Pa.   Contact: Archivist
Mail: Box 278
Bryn Athyn, Pa. 19009

Mon.—Fri. 8:00am—5:00pm   No fee
By appointment   Some restrictions

Size of Collection: Approx. 800 lin. ft.
Areas of Interest: The Archive is the official repository for records of the Academy of the New Church, the General Church of the New Jerusalem, and the Bryn Athyn Church. It also has records from the various General Church societies throughout the world, from individuals associated with the Academy or Church organizations (personal papers), and materials regarding other New Church organizations or individuals.
Women's Material: Approx. 10 percent of total. The most significant is in three general categories: The Academy Girls' School records; the Bryn Athyn Church Women's Guild and Chancel Guild; and Theta Alpha (a church women's group). The Archive also has a collection of personal papers, the most important of which are those of Lillian Beekman, Alice Grant, Mary Leather Hyatt, and Laura Vickroy. The collection includes late nineteenth- and twentieth-century printed and handwritten material in the following areas:

Domestic Activity   Sciences
Education   Social Life
Literature   Work
Religion

See Hinding 14,730–14,735

AGNES IRWIN SCHOOL   PRosI

Independent School for Girls
Founded 1869

Ithan Avenue   (215) 525–8400
Rosemont, Pa. 19010   Contact: Librarian

School Days 7:00am–4:00pm   No fee
By appointment   Some restrictions

Size of Collection: NA

Areas of Interest: Books and other materials relating to the school and its founder, Agnes Irwin (1841–1914). The School, founded as Penn Square Seminary, claims to be the oldest private girls' school in continuous existence in the United States.

Women's Material: 100 percent of total. Records of the School include historical scrapbooks from 1889 to 1969. The Library also has materials on Agnes Repplier (1855–1950).

THE AMERICAN COLLEGE   PBmAmC

Accredited Non-Traditional Institution Devoted to the Study of Life Insurance and the Related Financial Sciences, Archive, Museum
Founded 1927

270 Bryn Mawr Avenue   (215) 896–4506
Bryn Mawr, Pa. 19010   Contact: Director of Archives & Oral
                                      History

Mon.—Fri. 8:45am—4:30pm   No fee

Size of Collection: 100 oral history interviews, 50 lin. ft. museum, 75 cu. ft. papers.

Areas of Interest: History of the American College. The collection also has materials on the history of life insurance, the history of professional education in life insurance and the related financial sciences, and oral history interviews with life insurance professionals. The focus is national, 1927 to the present.

Women's Material: 1 percent overall, 10 percent of oral histories. The collection has ten oral history interviews, including transcripts, with professional women life insurance agents of the early 1930s. The College also has moden records of women professionals in life insurance and the related financial services devoted to the preservation of human life value.

AMERICAN FRIENDS SERVICE COMMITTEE   PPAmF

Social, Philanthropic Organization
Founded 1917

1501 Cherry Street   (215) 241–7044
Philadelphia, Pa. 19102   Contact: Archivist

Mon.—Fri. 8:00am—4:00pm   No fee
                                      Application with references required

Size of Collection: Approx. 2,000 lin. ft.
Areas of Interest: Records of the American Friends Service Committee from 1917 to the present.
Women's Material: Involvement of women in the activities of the Committee.

AMERICAN PHILOSOPHICAL SOCIETY LIBRARY   PPAmP

Library, Archive
Founded 1743

105 South 5th Street
Philadelphia, Pa. 19106

(215) 627–0706
Contact: Librarian

Mon.—Fri. 9:00am—5:00pm

No fee

Published Guides: *Archives and Manuscript Collections of the APS, Guide to Manuscripts Relating to the American Indian, Catalog of Portraits, Catalog of Instruments and Models.*
Size of Collection: 159,300 books, 5,125,000 manuscripts, 7,000 microfilms, also prints and photographs.
Areas of Interest: History of American science and technology, including related European background. The collection includes materials on Franklin, electricity, American Indian linguistics, Charles Darwin, evolution, genetics, biochemistry, and quantum physics.
Women's Material: Approx. 5 percent of total. Includes papers of Jane Aitken, Elsie Clews Parsons, Florence Sabin, Florence Seiber, and Grace E.B. Murphy. Family history can be found in the papers of the Hare-Willing family, Bache and Duane families, and Peale-Sellers families. Lydia Maria Child correspondence is in the J. Peter Lesley papers. M. Carey Thomas correspondence is in the Simon Flexner papers. The library also has biographical material on women members of the Society and women scientists, and printed reports from nineteenth-century Philadelphia area women's charity and relief organizations.

See Hinding 14,881–14,904

AMERICAN SWEDISH HISTORICAL FOUNDATION/MUSEUM   PPAmS

Museum, Library, Archive
Founded 1926

1900 Pattison Avenue
Philadelphia, Pa. 19145

(215) 389–1776
Contact: Exhibits & Program Director

Tues.—Fri. 10:00am—4:00pm
Sat. 12:00noon—4:00pm

Fee: $1.50 adults; $1.00 students
Library does not circulate except for
Interlibrary Loan

Size of Collection: Approx. 1,600 objects.
Areas of Interest: The purpose is to preserve the heritage of Swedes and other Scandinavians in America dating from the arrival of the Swedes in the Delaware Valley in 1638. In addition to maintaining a museum of fourteen galleries, the institution serves as a cultural center dedicated to promoting understanding between contemporary Scandinavian and American cultures.

Women's Material: Approx. 50 percent of total. Includes records on the activities of Queen Christina and Armegott Printz relating to New Sweden from 1638 to 1655. The archive has memorabilia, books, and letters of Fredrika Bremer (1801–1865), Swedish novelist and advocate for women's rights, who toured the United States from 1849 to 1851 and visited Philadelphia. Her travel logs comment on most aspects of American life of the mid-nineteenth century. The collection also has memorabilia, letters, and sheet music of Jenny Lind (1820–1887), Swedish opera singer who toured the United States, including Philadelphia, on various occasions. The Museum has Swedish and Swedish-American artifacts from 1600 to 1900 as follows:

Appliances and Equipment
Clothing and Accessories
Furniture
Household Items
Musical Instruments
Paintings
Photographs

Prints
Religious Artifacts
Scientific Apparatus
Sculpture
Textiles
Toys and Amusements

See Hinding 14,905–14,906

THE ATHENÆUM OF PHILADELPHIA   PPA

Library, Museum
Founded 1814

219 South 6th Street
Philadelphia, Pa. 19106

(215) 925–2688
Contact: Librarian

Mon.—Fri. 9:00am—5:00pm
Research by appointment

No fee

Size of Collection: 100,000 items.

Areas of Interest: Social and cultural history of the nineteenth century, including material up to 1930. Special areas of strength include architecture and decorative arts, early travel, domestic economy, the French in America, literature, and nineteenth-century periodicals.

Women's Material: 1 percent of total. The collection has Sarah J. Hale papers, ca. 1824 to 1860, including correspondence with Louis A. Godey, Lydia Sigourney, Emma Willard, Louisa Tuthill, etc. It also has biographical files on Philadelphia women architects and decorative arts renderings done by Rosamund Curzon while a student at Moore College of Art. The library has nineteenth-century books, periodicals, and monographs in the following areas:

Art, Architecture, Decorative Arts
Behavior
Domestic Activity

Literature
Sciences
Social Life

The collection also includes nineteenth- and twentieth-century European and American artifacts as follows:

Ceramics
Drawings
Furniture
Paintings and Sculpture

Photographs
Prints
Silver

25

Institutions

ATWATER KENT MUSEUM   PPAtK

History Museum of the City of Philadelphia
Founded 1939

15 South 7th Street
Philadelphia, Pa. 19106

(215) 686–3630
Contact: Curator

Tues.—Sat. 9:30am—5:00pm

No fee

Size of Collection: 10,000 prints, numerous objects.

Areas of Interest: Diverse collections include prints, photographs, scrapbooks, paintings, toys and dolls, costumes, trade signs, and household goods, covering 300 years of Philadelphia's history. The Museum also has the city's archaeological collection.

Women's Material: Approx. 10 percent of total. The collections of the Friends Historical Association include costumes and dolls of eighteenth- and nineteenth-century Quaker women. Household items, needlework, and graphic images useful as a resource on women's topics are contained in other collections. The Museum has printed and some audio/visual materials in the following areas:

Art, Architecture, Decorative Arts	Medicine
Behavior	Performing Arts
Charities	Religion
Domestic Activity	Social Life
Education	Technology
Literature	Work

It also has a large collection of artifacts:

Appliances and Equipment	Paintings
Clothing and Accessories	Photographs
Drawings	Religious Artifacts
Furniture	Textiles
Household Items	Toys and Amusements

THE BALCH INSTITUTE FOR ETHNIC STUDIES   PPBI

Library, Archive, Museum
Founded 1971

18 South 7th Street
Philadelphia, Pa. 19106

(215) 925–8090
Contact: Library Director

Mon.—Sat. 9:00am—5:00pm

No fee
Library does not circulate except for
Interlibrary Loan

Size of Collection: 50,000 vols., thousands of photos, hundreds of sound recordings.

Areas of Interest: Collections of printed, archival, manuscript, pictorial, and aural materials documenting the experience of immigrants to North America and their descendants. The primary emphasis of the collection is on the nineteenth and twentieth centuries. The library is not only interested in immigration to North America, but also in the return by immigrants and/or their descendants to their country of origin. Any subsequent emigration from the United States or Canada to another country is also of importance.

Women's Material: 5 percent of total. Includes the Magdalen Society records and papers of Marion E. Potts, Anna Boyko, and Wadeeha Atiyeh. The Institute also has the papers of Rose I. Bender, a Philadelphia-born Zionist of Lithuanian parentage. The Bender Papers include correspondence, clippings, and miscellaneous items relating to her activities in Hadassah, the Zionist Organization of the American Allied Jewish Appeal, and other Jewish concerns such as the National Jewish Hospital. The Institute has printed and some handwritten and machine-readable material in the areas listed. Most is from the nineteenth and twentieth centuries, some from the eighteenth.

Art, Architecture, Decorative Arts

Domestic Activity

Education

Feminism and Reform

Law

Literature

Minorities and Ethnicity

Performing Arts

Religion

Social Life

Work

The collection also includes two paintings and several hundred twentieth-century photographs.

See Hinding 14,907–14,910

BISHOP'S MILL HISTORICAL INSTITUTE—COLONIAL PENNSYLVANIA PLANTATION, SOL FEINSTONE LIBRARY   PEdB

Library, Museum
Founded 1973

P.O. Box 385
Edgemont, Pa. 19028

(215) 353–1777
Contact: Executive Secretary

Library: April—Nov.
Mon.—Thurs. 9:00am—2:00pm
By appointment
Museum: Tues.—Fri. 9:00am—2:00pm
Sat., Sun. 10:00am—4:00pm
Tours and workshops by appointment

Fee: $2.00 Adults; $1.00 Senior Citizens

Size of Collection: 1,500 books, 500 bound periodicals, 125 reels microfilm of county records, 25 local maps, 25 architectural drawings.

Areas of Interest: Living history eighteenth-century working farm which replicates eighteenth-century life through experimentation and use of old tools. The Institute has some extensive research on crafts, clothing, food, etc.

Women's Material: Records of experiments made by women volunteers on food processing, clothing, crafts, farm chores, etc. There are also secondary sources in the library. Female interpreters on the education staff are excellent sources. The Institute has material in the following areas:

Art, Architecture, and Decorative Arts

Behavior

Domestic Activity

Medicine

It also has artifacts from 1760 to 1790:

Clothing and Accessories

Furniture

Household Items

Textiles

BORDENTOWN HISTORICAL SOCIETY NjBHi

Historical Society
Founded 1930

14 Crosswicks Street
Bordentown, N.J. 08505

(609) 298–1740
Contact: Docent in charge of Headquarters

Mon.—Fri. 10:00am—4:00pm

No fee

Size of Collection: NA
Areas of Interest: NA
Women's Material: Includes paintings by Susan Waters, wax miniatures by Patience Wright, and papers of Clara Barton. The Society also has some clothing and accessories.

BRANDYWINE RIVER MUSEUM PChB

Library, Museum
Founded 1971

P.O. Box 141
Chadds Ford, Pa. 19317

(215) 388–7601
Contact: Curator of Collections

Mon.—Sun. 9:30am—4:30pm
By appointment for library and paintings not on display

Fee: $1.75 Adults

Size of Collection: 700 paintings; 2,500 books and periodicals.
Areas of Interest: Works of art by illustrator Howard Pyle and his over 150 students, also works by N. C., Andrew, and Jamie Wyeth, and drawings, etchings, and landscape paintings by local artists. The majority of the work is from the period 1875 to 1945 with the exception of Andrew and Jamie Wyeth. Library holdings include illustrated books and periodicals 1875 to 1940.
Women's Material: 25 percent of total. Illustrations by women artists working in Philadelphia, including drawings, paintings, photographs, and prints. The collection has copies of books and magazines illustrated by women, indexed by artists' names and original photographs and letters of Philadelphia illustrator Charlotte Harding (Brown) 1873 to 1951.

BRYN MAWR COLLEGE—ARCHIVE PBm-A

College Archive and Manuscript Collection
College founded 1885

Bryn Mawr, Pa. 19010

(215) 645–5285/5289
Contact: College Archivist

Mon.—Fri. 9:00am—4:00pm

No fee
Restrictions vary according to collection

Published Guides: *Guide to the Microfilm of the Papers of M. Carey Thomas in the Bryn Mawr College Archives.*

Size of Collection: Approx. 2,250 ft.

Areas of Interest: Bryn Mawr College records and the history of women, chiefly in the Philadelphia area.

Women's Material: 98 percent of total. The collections include: papers of college presidents M. Carey Thomas, Marion E. Park, and Katherine McBride, as well as other records relating to the history of the college. The archive also has correspondence of Caroline H. Dall, Dorothy North Haskins, and Marianne Moore, the Katharine Sergeant White *New Yorker* papers, the C. C. Catt collection, and others. The Archives have printed, handwritten, and some machine-readable and audio/visual material from 1885 to the present in the following areas:

Art, Architecture, Decorative Arts	Performing Arts
Charities	Religion
Education	Sciences
Feminism and Reform	Social Work
Literature	Work

The collection also has artifacts from the same period:

Clothing and Accessories	Photographs
Drawings	Prints
Paintings	Scientific Apparatus

See Hinding 14,736–14,745

BRYN MAWR COLLEGE—LIBRARY   PBm-L

College Library
College founded 1885

Bryn Mawr, Pa. 19010

(215) 645–5275
Contact: Head, Public Services

Mon.—Fri. 8:00am—4:00pm

No fee
Reference use by adults

Size of Collection: 759,000 vols.

Areas of Interest: The general College Library has materials, chiefly of a scholarly nature, on all phases of women's lives and contributions, past and present. In addition, there is representative non-scholarly material of historical and sociological interest.

Women's Material: 4 percent of total (see above). The Library has the 1,248 reel *History of Women* microfilm collection of almost 12,000 volumes and over 2,000 periodicals, manuscripts, and photographs from the Schlesinger Library on the History of Women (Radcliffe), the Sophia Smith Collection, and several other libraries. Bryn Mawr's own collection includes much non-American material from the sixteenth century on, not included in the microfilm. There are also considerable holdings on women's higher education. The reference collection has most of the significant bibliographies and other reference tools in the field of women's studies. The Library has nineteenth- and twentieth-century material in the following areas:

Art, Architecture, Decorative Arts	Minorities and Ethnicity
Behavior	Performing Arts
Charities	Religion
Domestic Activity	Sciences

Education
Feminism and Reform
Law
Literature
Medicine

Sex
Social Life
Statistics
Technology
Work

BURLINGTON COUNTY HISTORICAL SOCIETY   NJBuHi

Historical Society, Library, Archive, Museum
Founded 1915

457 High Street
Burlington, N.J. 08016

(609) 386–4773
Contact: Administrator

Wed. 1:00pm—4:00pm
Sun. 2:00pm—4:00pm

$1.00 Contribution
Does not circulate

Size of Collection: 20,000 objects.
Areas of Interest: Burlington County history, artifacts, buildings, manuscripts; also New Jersey history and genealogy.
Women's Material: 40 percent of total. Handwritten diaries of Grace Moore, 1880 to 1890; quilts with genealogical information; clothing identifiable to its owner; wedding certificates; and manumission records. The collection also has the Revolutionary War Journal of Margaret Morris and personal letters of five women. The Society holds primarily nineteenth-century printed and handwritten materials in the following areas:

Behavior
Charities
Domestic Activity
Education
Feminism and Reform
Law
Literature
Medicine

Performing Arts
Religion
Sex
Social Life
Statistics
Technology
Work

It also has artifacts as follows:

Appliances and Equipment
Clothing and Accessories
Drawings
Household Items

Paintings
Photographs
Textiles
Toys and Amusements

BUTEN MUSEUM OF WEDGWOOD   PMeB

Museum
Founded 1957

246 North Bowman Avenue
Merion, Pa. 19066

(215) 664–6601
Contact: Director

Tues.—Fri. 2:00pm—5:00pm
Sat. 10:00am—1:00pm

Fee: $1.50

Size of Collection: 10,000 items.

Areas of Interest: English ceramics, especially pieces made by Wedgwood.
Women's Material: Some pieces designed by women, some portraying women, many used by women.

CABRINI COLLEGE LIBRARY   PRCL

College Library
College founded 1957

Eagle Road   (215) 687–2100
Radnor, Pa. 19087   Contact: Library Director

Mon.—Thurs. 8:30am—10:00pm   No fee
Fri. 8:30am—5:00pm   Some restrictions
Weekends during academic year

Size of Collection: 70,000 vols.
Areas of Interest: General college collection for use of faculty and students.
Women's Material: Includes works on the history and social conditions of women from revolutionary America to the present. The Library also has material on women and theology and a large number of biographies. It houses two closed collections: the Cabriniana Collection of primary and secondary information on Saint Frances Cabrini; and the College Archives, including material on the Missionary Sisters of the Sacred Heart (founded 1880) as well as College departments, publications, and news releases.

CAMDEN COUNTY HISTORICAL SOCIETY   NjCHi

Library, Archive, Museum, Historic House
Founded 1899

Park Boulevard and Euclid Avenue   (609) 964–3333
Camden, N.J. 08103   Contact: Director; Librarian

Mon.—Thurs. 12:30pm—4:30pm   No fee
Sun. 2:00pm—4:30pm   Does not circulate

Size of Collection: 18,000 vols., plus maps, photos, genealogy.
Areas of Interest: History of Camden County, New Jersey, Delaware, Philadelphia, Pennsylvania, New York. The Society has materials on genealogy, biography, and decorative arts, 1681 to the present.
Women's Material: Includes records of the Women's Club of Camden, 1894 to 1960, biographies, oral histories, diaries, reminiscences, memory books, and letters. The Society also has records of the Camden Equal Suffrage League, 1916 to 1923. The collection includes nineteenth- and twentieth-century printed, handwritten, machine-readable and audio/visual materials in the following areas:

Domestic Activity   Sex
Feminism and Reform   Social Life
Performing Arts

The Society also maintains an eighteenth-century furnished house and has numerous nineteenth- and twentieth-century photographs.

See Hinding 10,891

CHESTER COUNTY HISTORICAL SOCIETY   PWcHi

Library, Archive, Museum
Founded 1893

225 North High Street
West Chester, Pa. 19380

(215) 692–4800
Contact: Librarian; Curator of Collections

Library/Museum: Tues., Thurs., Fri.
10:00am—4:00pm;   Wed.   1:00pm—
8:00pm
Library only: Sat. 10:00am—4:00pm

Fee: $2.00 adults; $1.00 senior citizens;
$.50 children & students
Some restrictions

Size of Collection: NA
Areas of Interest: Property and information of historic value or interest to the people of Chester County. The museum concentrates on paintings, needlework, weaving, costumes, and accessories. The library's concentration is in printed books, manuscripts, photographs, maps, and microfilm.
Women's Material: Includes needlework of the eighteenth and nineteenth centuries, samplers, pocketbooks, quilts, and some handwoven coverlets made and/or used by women in Chester County and the Delaware Valley.

See Hinding 15,338—15,346

CHESTNUT HILL COLLEGE—ARCHIVES   PPCCH

Archive (See also Sisters of St. Joseph)
Founded 1924

Germantown and Northwestern Avenues
Philadelphia, Pa. 19118

(215) 248–7054
Contact: Librarian

Mon.—Thurs. 9:00am—2:00pm
By appointment

No fee

Size of Collection: 130 cu. ft.
Areas of Interest: Materials relating to the development of Chestnut Hill College from its founding in 1924 to the present. Included are college catalogues, student publications, information on curriculum changes, etc. The Sisters of St. Joseph archive has additional materials on the founding of the college.
Women's Material: 95 percent of total. Records relating to the history of a liberal arts college for women. The collection includes numerous photographs, some textiles, and several children's handwork books.

See Hinding 14,911

CHEYNEY STATE COLLEGE—LESLIE PINCKNEY HILL LIBRARY   PCSC

Library
College founded as the Institute for Colored Youth, 1852

Cheyney State College
Cheyney, Pa. 19319

(215) 758–2208
Contact: Director

Fri. 8:30am—5:00pm; Sat. 9:00am—
    3:00pm; Sun. 4:00pm—10:00pm

Size of Collection: 133,000 items.

Areas of Interest: To support the academic programs of a four-year liberal arts college and a master's program in education.

Women's Material: Less than 1 percent of total. The records of the Institute for Colored Youth include material on a number of women. The general collection has books on the following topics:

Art, Architecture, Decorative Arts	Medicine
Charities	Minorities and Ethnicity
Education	Religion
Feminism and Reform	Sciences
Law	Work
Literature	

CHRIST CHURCH, PHILADELPHIA   PPChC

Church
Founded 1695

2nd Street above Market   (215) 922–1695
Philadelphia, Pa. 19106   Contact: Rector

Mon.—Fri. 9:00am—4:30pm   No fee
                                Only microfilm records may be used

Published Guides: *Guide to Microfilm of the Records of Christ Church, Philadelphia.*

Size of Collection: 25,000 items.

Areas of Interest: The history of Christ Church is in the Archives. The Bray Library, housed at the Library Company of Philadelphia, has early eighteenth-century religious works.

Women's Material: Records of some of the women who made possible the survival of Christ Church parish before and after the War of Independence.

CITY ARCHIVES OF PHILADELPHIA   PPCA

Archive
Founded 1952

523 City Hall Annex   (215) 686–2276
Philadelphia, Pa. 19107   Contact: City Archivist

Mon.—Fri. 8:30am—5:00pm exc. city   No fee
    holidays   Some current records only with
                                  permission

Published Guides: *Descriptive Inventory of the Archives of the City and County of Philadelphia; Subject Index to the Photograph Collection of the Philadelphia City Archives.*

Size of Collection: 20,000 cu. ft.

Areas of Interest: Records originating from operations or activities of the city and county governments of Philadelphia, 1682 to the present.

Women's Material: 9 percent of total. Includes the records of the Guardians of the Poor, Bureau of Charities, and Department of Public Health relating to female inmates of the Alms House and patients of Philadelphia General Hospital, and records of the Inspectors of the Jail and Penitentiary House and Inspectors of the County Prison pertaining to female inmates. The Archives also have records of the Women's Centennial Executive Committee and Annual Reports, 1875–1877. Many records series, such as deeds, tax lists, and birth, death, and marriage records include information about women. Materials are both printed and handwritten.

*See Hinding 14,912–14,924**

CLIVEDEN   PPCl

Museum
House built 1763–1767, Museum founded 1972

6401 Germantown Avenue
Philadelphia, Pa. 19144

Tues.—Sat. 10:00am—4:00pm
Sun. 1:00pm—4:30pm

(215) 848–1777
Contact: Executive Director

Fee: $2.00 adults, $1.50 senior citizens,
   $1.00 students
Use by permission

Size of Collection: 25,000 items.

Areas of Interest: Cliveden serves as a continuing-history house museum covering the period from 1763 to 1972, and is a co-stewardship property of the National Trust for Historic Preservation operated by Cliveden, Inc. The collection, primarily made up of Chew Family pieces, features outstanding examples of Philadelphia-Chippendale and -Federal furnishings. (The builder of the house was Chief Justice Benjamin Chew.) An excellent example of domestic American Mid-Georgian architecture, the house was the site of the pivotal action of the Battle of Germantown (Oct. 4, 1777).

Women's Material: 1 percent of total. Includes women's clothing (a collection of late eighteenth- and nineteenth-century formal as well as everyday wear and cotton house dresses), domestic furnishings, and implements. Cliveden also has some paintings, photographs, prints, sculptures, and textiles.

COLLEGE OF PHYSICIANS OF PHILADELPHIA   PPC

Professional Association, Library, Archive, Museum
Founded 1787

19 South 22nd Street
Philadelphia, Pa. 19103

Mon.—Fri. 9:00am—5:00pm

(215) 561–6050
Contact: Director of Library

No fee
Does not circulate

Size of Collection: 350,000 vols.

Areas of Interest: Medical and scientific, with an emphasis on surgery, dermatology, obstetrics, gynecology, pediatrics, medical history, and general medicine.

Women's Material: Books, periodicals, monographs, etc. in obstetrics and gynecology, nursing, and medicine in general. The College also has some objects relating to women in the museum collection, and papers of women physicians.

See Hinding 14,925–14,928

THE COSMOPOLITAN CLUB OF PHILADELPHIA, INC.   PPCos

Women's Social Club
Founded 1928

1616 Latimer Street
Philadelphia, Pa. 19103

(215) 735–1057
Contact: Archivist

Mon.—Fri. 9:00am—5:00pm

No fee
Use by permission of Board

Size of Collection: NA
Areas of Interest: Records of the Club.
Women's Material: Board minutes and archives dealing with the history of the Club's development since its founding. The outstanding ability of the Club to attract nationally notable speakers over the years results in an interesting guest book and small archival collection. The library contains members' published works, some of which were introduced at the clubhouse.

THE CURTIS INSTITUTE OF MUSIC LIBRARY   PPCI

Music Institute Library
Institute founded 1924

Knapp Hall
1720 Locust Street
Philadelphia, Pa. 19103

(215) 893–5265
Contact: Librarian

Mon.—Fri. 9:00am—5:00pm
By appointment

No fee

Size of Collection: 50,000 vols.
Areas of Interest: Primarily music scores (concert literature for traditional instruments), 4,000 recordings, 40 journal subscriptions. The archives of the Institute include scrapbooks and photographs, as well as clippings, programs, and recordings of Curtis recitals.
Women's Material: 5 percent of total. Includes photographs, some letters and personal papers of Mary Louise Curtis Bok Zimbalist, founder of the Institute. The library also has materials on the published accomplishments (including recordings) of alumnae, many of whom are well-known performers.

DELAWARE COUNTY HISTORICAL SOCIETY   PCDHi

Library, Archive
Founded 1895

Wolfgram Memorial Library
Widener University
Chester, Pa. 19013

(215) 874–6444
Contact: Curator

Mon.—Fri. 10:00am—3:00pm
First Sun. of month 1:00pm—5:00pm

Fee: $1.00 for non-members
Does not circulate

Published Guides: *Pennsylvania Newspapers Bibliography and Union List;* occasional bulletins.

Size of Collection: 6,000 vols., 300 microfilm reels, 60 document drawers.

Areas of Interest: The main concentration is on Delaware County history, colonial Pennsylvania, Philadelphia, and neighboring counties, colonial to the present. The Society also holds genealogical records.

Women's Material: Works of local women historians, scrapbooks of Dr. Anna Broomall, photographs of Louise Deshong Woodbridge, and writings of Christine and Elizabeth Morley. The Society also has some nursing documents.

DELAWARE DIVISION OF HISTORICAL AND CULTURAL AFFAIRS— ARCHIVES BRANCH   DeDHi-A

Archives
Founded 1905

Hall of Records
Dover, Del. 19901

(302) 736–5318
Contact: Archivist

Tues.—Fri. 8:30am—12:00noon,
    1:00pm—4:15pm;   Sat.   8:00am—
    12:30pm; 1:00pm—3:45pm

No fee

Size of Collection: NA

Areas of Interest: All non-current records of the State of Delaware, its counties and large municipalities, from 1638 to the present. The Archives also include genealogical records and a manuscript collection.

Women's Material: Records series, such as judicial papers, deeds, wills, vital statistics files, etc. include information about women.

DIOCESE OF PENNSYLVANIA, PROTESTANT EPISCOPAL CHURCH   PPPE

Church Archive
Diocese founded 1784, Archive founded 1841

425 Lombard Street
Philadelphia, Pa. 19147
(temporary address)

(215) 627–1852
Contact: Archivist

Mon.—Fri. 9:00am—5:00pm

No fee
Restriction policy in process of development

Size of Collection: 200 cu. ft.

Areas of Interest: Consist primarily of the official records of the Diocese of Pennsylvania of the Protestant Episcopal Church since 1784. Originally comprising the entire state, the Diocese was by divisions (1865, 1871) reduced to the five counties of Bucks, Montgomery, Philadelphia, Delaware, and Chester. Records of the Convention, the bishops, the Standing Committee, and other committees, commissions, and organizations of the Diocese, or affiliated with the Diocese, and records of closed parishes are collected. Internal diocesan affairs, missionary outreach, charitable activities, and the interaction of church and society are documented.

Women's Material: 9 percent of total. Records and correspondence of individuals and of organizations in which women participated and exercised significant leadership. The archive includes material on: the Woman's Auxiliary/Episcopal Churchwomen, the Indian's Hope Association, and the Elizabeth Price Martin Fellowship; the work of deaconesses and the ordination of women, The Church Training and Deaconess House, and the Bishop Memorial House (a sisterhood of deaconesses); The Episcopal Female Tract Society, The Bishop White Parish Library Association, The Church School Service League, and the Episcopal Hospital Mission; charitable and service organizations such as The Sheltering Arms, St. Martha's House, Church Mission of Help, St. Stephen's Serviceman's Center and the Diocesan War Commission (World War II). The collection has nineteenth- and twentieth-century printed and handwritten documents on charities, education, and religion, as well as some photographs.

DOMINICAN SISTERS: CONGREGATION OF SAINT CATHERINE DE' RICCI   PEIDS

Congregation of Religious Women
Founded in Philadelphia 1901

Archives   (215) 635–4540
St. Catherine's Hall   Contact: Archivist
Elkins Park, Pa. 19117

Mon.—Tues. 10:00am—4:30pm   No fee
(may vary)   Does not circulate

Size of Collection: 161 lin. ft.

Areas of Interest: Records of the Congregation. Founded in 1880 and established in Philadelphia in 1901, the Dominican Sisters were American pioneers in retreats for women. The records document the development of Christian women through retreats and the massive migration of young women to the cities, 1901 to the present. By providing accessibility of a Christian environment and special services to the American working woman through educational opportunities, lectures, libraries, moral formation, creative use of leisure, and development of the whole person, the Order gave new thrusts toward independence and self-fulfillment of women.

Women's Material: 100 percent of total. Includes the Annual Report of the Catholic Guild, 1898, 1901, 1902, 1903, 1904 and accounts of Mother M. Gregory Gagan (1901–1954), Mother M. Emmanuel (1932–1966), and Sister M. Raphael Stanley (1932–1975). The collection has three theses regarding social aspects of residence ministry in Philadelphia, 1959, 1961, 1964; a brief history of the foundress, 1949; and a brief history of the Congregation, 1980. The archive also has numerous magazine and newspaper articles on works of the Congregation and numerous pictures.

*See Hinding 14,783**

DREXEL UNIVERSITY LIBRARY PPD-L

Library
University founded 1891

32nd and Chestnut Streets (215) 895–2755
Philadelphia, Pa. 19104 Contact: Drexel Collection Librarian

Mon.—Fri. 9:00am—5:00pm No fee
Use in library building only, some
photocopies permitted

Size of Collection: Approx. 3,500 vols., plus misc. pamphlet material.

Areas of Interest: The archives collection pertains to Drexel University, 1891 to the present; the Drexel family, including genealogy beginning in the eighteenth century; and Drexel faculty and alumni.

Women's Material: Approx. 10 percent of total. Includes Drexel Women's Club materials; Masters and Doctoral theses by women students; alumni materials; faculty and alumnae monographs; photographs related to the University; and papers pertaining to the Pennsylvania Library Club (1901–1938). Theses and monographs cover art, architecture, decorative arts; behavior; domestic activity; education; literature; sciences; religion; social life; library science.

See Hinding 14,929–14,931

DREXEL UNIVERSITY MUSEUM COLLECTION PPD-M

Museum
Founded 1891

32nd and Chestnut Streets (215) 895–2424
Philadelphia, Pa. 19104 Contact: Director and Curator

Mon.—Fri. 10:00am—4:00pm No fee

Published Guides: Checklist of nineteenth-century paintings.

Size of Collection: 7,000 items.

Areas of Interest: Objects made or collected during the nineteenth century, including paintings, sculpture, decorative arts, documentary photographs, costumes, and other ethnographic materials. The Museum also has a collection of late nineteenth- and twentieth-century miniatures.

Women's Material: 30–40 percent of total. Includes works by Cecilia Beaux, Violet Oakley, and Margaret Wasserman Levy. The collection also has photographs of Drexel students. The Museum has nineteenth- and twentieth-century art and artifacts as follows:

Clothing and Accessories	Photographs
Drawings	Sculpture
Furniture	Textiles
Paintings	Toys and Amusements

DROPSIE COLLEGE LIBRARY   PPDrop

Library, Archive
College founded 1905

Broad and York Streets	(215) 229–0110
Philadelphia, Pa. 19132	Contact: Library Director
Mon.—Fri. 9:00am—4:30pm	Free
	No loans

Published Guides: To some special collections, e.g. Isaac Leeser, Mayer Sulzberger.
Size of Collection: 150,000 vols.
Areas of Interest: Rabbinic literature, Biblical and post-Biblical learning, Semitic language, Assyriology, Egyptology, Ancient Near East, Jewish and Middle Eastern studies.
Women's Material: Less than 1 percent of total. Works dealing with women in Jewish law and Jewish life.

EDUCATIONAL TESTING SERVICE   NjPETS

Non-Profit Educational, Measurement, and Research Organization
Founded 1947

ETS Archives 30-B	(609) 734–5744
Princeton, N.J. 08541	Contact: Archivist
Mon.—Fri. 8:30am—4:45pm	No fee
	Most primary source documents restricted

Size of Collection: 1,000 cu. ft.
Areas of Interest: Documents relevant to the history of the Educational Testing Service. All material is from the twentieth century.
Women's Material: (Unrestricted) Includes research studies and other publications concerning sex differences in test performance, sex bias in testing, women's education, sex discrimination, cognitive styles, menstruation, women prisoners, women in the workplace, women's experiential learning, women students. The collection includes twentieth-century printed and some audio/visual material in the following areas:

Domestic Activity	Psychology
Education	Statistics—Test Results
Minorities and Ethnicity	Work
Performing Arts	

The Service also has some photographs.

See Hinding 11,150

ELEUTHERIAN MILLS HISTORICAL LIBRARY   DeGE

Library, Archive (see also Hagley Museum)
Founded as the Longwood Library in 1957

P.O. Box 3630
Greenville
Wilmington, Del. 19807

(302) 658–2400
Contact: Research & Reference Librarian

Mon.—Fri. 8:30am—4:30pm
2nd Sat. of month 9:00am—4:30pm

No fee
Time seal, Donor restrictions

Published Guides: *Guide to Manuscripts in the Eleutherian Mills Historical Library; Supplement to the Guide to Manuscripts.*
Size of Collection: 150,000 vols., 15 million mss. items.
Areas of Interest: Manuscripts, archives, imprints, and pictures illustrative of the industrial and technological history of the Delaware Valley region, 1700 to 1920, with special concentration in the nineteenth century.
Women's Material: Approx. 5 percent of total. Papers of the women of the du Pont family, papers of early women of the Lukens family (sparse). The Library has eighteenth-, nineteenth-, and twentieth-century printed and handwritten materials in the following areas:

Army Life
Daily Life
1838/39 Trip to Cuba

Social Life
Work

See Hinding 2,028–2,033

THE EMERGENCY AID OF PENNSYLVANIA   PPEmA

Women's Charitable Organization
Founded 1914

1629 Locust Street
Philadelphia, Pa. 19103

(215) 545–0730
Contact: President

By appointment

No fee

Size of Collection: NA
Areas of Interest: Records of the organization.
Women's Material: Records of women's charitable organization founded in 1914 to do war relief work.

FEDERAL ARCHIVES AND RECORDS CENTER   PPFA

Archive
Founded 1971

5000 Wissahickon Avenue
Philadelphia, Pa. 19144

(215) 951–5591
Contact: Chief, Archives Branch

Mon.—Fri. 7:30am—4:00pm

No fee
Some record groups restricted

Published Guides: *Research Sources in the Archives Branch of the Philadelphia Federal Archives and Records Center.*
Size of Collection: 35,000 cu. ft.
Areas of Interest: Records of Federal offices within Pennsylvania, Delaware, Maryland, Virginia, and West Virginia, 1789 to 1976.
Women's Material: The Center has no series dealing specifically with women. However, women are included in many record groups, such as suits in Federal court cases, etc.

See Hinding 14,932–14,939

FIRST AFRICAN UNITED PRESBYTERIAN CHURCH PPFAf

Church
Founded 1807

4159 Girard Avenue   (215) 477–3100
Philadelphia, Pa. 19104   Contact: Pastor

By appointment   No fee

Size of Collection: NA
Areas of Interest: Records of the oldest black Presbyterian church in the world, founded 1807. The Church also has articles donated 1910 to the present.
Women's Material: Minute book of the Ladies Gloucester Memorial Society, 1910 to 1925. The Church also has correspondence and some twentieth-century textiles and porcelain.

SAMUEL S. FLEISHER ART MEMORIAL PPFl

Museum (Sanctuary), Art Center with classes and gallery
(Administered by Philadelphia Museum of Art)
Founded 1898 as the Graphic Sketch Club

709–721 Catharine Street   (215) 922–3456
Philadelphia, Pa. 19147   Contact: Administrator

Mon.—Thurs. 12:00noon—5:00pm;   No fee
   7:00pm—9:30pm; Oct.—June
Appointment required to view
   Sanctuary

Published Guides: *History of the Samuel S. Fleisher Art Memorial.*
Size of Collection: 200 works.
Areas of Interest: Objects appropriate for installation in the Sanctuary or other permanent exhibition areas. The Memorial has ceased acquisition.
Women's Material: 10 percent of total. Includes Violet Oakley's "Scenes from the Life of Moses," a reredos in the Sanctuary commissioned by Samuel S. Fleisher in memory of his mother. The museum also has drawings, paintings, prints, and religious artifacts by women.

THE FRANKLIN INSTITUTE SCIENCE MUSEUM PPF

Library, Archive, Museum
Founded 1824

20th Street and the Parkway
Philadelphia, Pa. 19103

(215) 448–1443
Contact: Curatorial Associate

Museum: Mon.—Sat. 10:00am—5:00pm;
  Sun. 12:00noon—5:00pm
Library: Mon.—Fri. 10:00am—5:00pm;
  by appointment

Fee: $3.50 adults; $3.00 students; $2.00
  senior citizens; $25.00/day use of
  Library by non-members

Published Guides: *Technology in Industrial America: The Committee on Science
and the Arts of the Franklin Institute, 1824–1900.*
Size of Collection: NA
Areas of Interest: Science and technology, concentrating on the Philadelphia area
from the establishment of The Franklin Institute in 1824 to date.
Women's Material: Approx. 1 percent of total. Includes records of the establishment of the School of Design for Women (now Moore College of Art) 1850–1853.
The archive also has material on women inventors and entrepreneurs in records of
the Committee on Exhibitions and Committee on Science and the Arts, 1824–1900.

See Hinding 14,940–14,943

FREE LIBRARY OF PHILADELPHIA PP

Library
Founded 1891

Logan Square
Philadelphia, Pa. 19103

(215) 686–5322

Mon.—Wed. 9:00am—9:00pm;
  Thurs.—Fri. 9:00am—6:00pm;
Sat. 9:00am–5:00pm;
Sunday hours during winter

No fee
Reference materials do not circulate

Published Guides: *Resource Guide 6: Women and Women's Issues,* a.o.
Size of Collection: 2,947,727 vols.
Areas of Interest: Materials on all subjects useful to the general public in their
day-to-day information needs.
Women's Material: Includes standard biographies, histories, bibliographical, and
other reference works.

FREE PUBLIC LIBRARY—TRENTON, NEW JERSEY NjT

Library
Founded 1750

120 Academy Street
Trenton, N.J. 08608

(609) 392–7188
Contact: Head of Reference Department

Mon., Wed., Thurs. 9:00am—9:00pm; No fee
  Tues., Fri., Sat. 9:00am—5:00pm
Research by appointment

Published Guides: Included in *Guide to Historical Manuscripts in New Jersey History* (forthcoming).

Size of Collection: 4,000 books; 403 bound magazines; 26 vf drawers of photographs; 34 miscellaneous vf; 28 reels of microfilm; maps, manuscripts.

Areas of Interest: Local history books, memorabilia, maps, pictures (historical and contemporary documentation of the city), and forty-seven oral history tapes. The library solicits records of local organizations if of general interest. The collection includes an index of newspapers for local people, events, trends, buildings, parks, etc. Trenton newspapers are on microfilm.

Women's Material: Includes records of the Trenton College Club, Zonta, and Delta Kappa Gamma Society, International and index cards listing sources of information for other local women's clubs. The library also has the Chesterfield Monthly Meeting Women's Minutes (Quaker) of 1688–1739, 1761–1786, 1790–1792, 1783–1824, 1827–1878 and records of Quaker marriages 1684–1847. Important local women are listed by name in the biography index and are in the picture file by name under individuals or as part of a group.

See Hinding 11,183–11,184

FRIENDS FREE LIBRARY OF GERMANTOWN PPFr

Library
Founded 1874

5418 Germantown Avenue (215) 438–6023
Philadelphia, Pa. 19144 Contact: Head Librarian

Mon.—Fri. 9:00am—4:00pm; No fee
  Sat. 9:00am—12:00noon
By appointment

Size of Collection: 55,000 vols.

Areas of Interest: Free public library supported by Germantown Monthly Meeting, with books of interest to general readers. It also serves as the school library for Germantown Friends School. Some emphasis is on such Quaker concerns as Indian rights, black history, Quaker history, and Germantown history.

Women's Material: Secondary research materials on women in Quakerism. The Library has the collection of Irvin C. Poley Theater Books: 250 bound scrapbooks of clippings of reviews, criticism, biographies, etc.; playbills, broadsides of theater productions in Philadelphia attended by Poley, 1900 to 1972 (indexed). It also has the archives of Germantown Friends School, a co-educational school, grades one to twelve, founded 1845: student publications, photographs, record books, etc.

GERMANTOWN HISTORICAL SOCIETY PPGHi

Library, Archive, 4 Museums: Agricultural and Domestic Tools; Costume; Decorative Arts; Toys, Dolls, and Quilts
Founded as the Site and Relic Society of Germantown 1900

5214 Germantown Avenue (215) 844–0514
Philadelphia, Pa. 19144 Contact: Director

Tues., Thurs. 10:00am—4:00pm; Fee: $1.00
Sun. 1:00pm—5:00pm
Archives by appointment only

Size of Collection: 5,000 vols.; approx. 50,000 papers; 1,000 photos; 60,000 museum objects.

Areas of Interest: Library and Archive: local history and genealogy, regional as secondary emphasis. Museums: Agricultural and domestic tools—local use or manufacture, 1750 to 1900; Costume—local use or manufacture, 1750 to 1950; Decorative Arts—local use or manufacture, 1683 to 1900; Toys, dolls, and quilts—local use or manufacture, 1800 to 1950.

Women's Material: Library, 5 percent or less; Archive, 5 percent or less; Agricultural and domestic tools, 10 percent or less; Costumes, 95 percent or more; Decorative Arts, 10 percent or less; Toys, dolls, and quilts, 95 percent or more. Includes an excellent collection of costumes and needlework, particularly quilts, samplers, dolls, and dollhouses. The Society has eighteenth-, nineteenth-, and twentieth-century printed and handwritten materials in the following areas:

Charities Local Horticultural Societies
Education Religion
Literature Sciences
Local Civic Associations Social Life

It also has eighteenth-, nineteenth-, and twentieth-century artifacts as follows:

Appliances and Equipment Photographs
Clothing and Accessories Textiles
Household Items Toys and Amusements
Paintings

See Hinding 14,944

GIRL SCOUTS OF GREATER PHILADELPHIA PPGS

Service Organization for Girls, ages 6 to 17
Founded 1917

7 Benjamin Franklin Parkway (215) 564–4657
Philadelphia, Pa. 19103 Contact: Chairman of Archives
Committee

Mon.—Fri. 8:30am—6:00pm No fee
No circulation

Size of Collection: NA
Areas of Interest: Material covers the history and activities of the Philadelphia Council of Girl Scouts from its incorporation in 1917. The local office has some material concerning the national scope of the organization.

Women's Material: 100 percent of total. Includes a complete set of all handbooks ever published for girls' use in developing programs for their troops. The organization also has a collection of all the uniforms ever worn by Girl Scouts from 1912 on as well as many photographs, 1917 to the present.

GLASSBORO STATE COLLEGE—SAVITZ LIBRARY, SPECIAL COLLECTIONS (Stewart Room)   NjGbS

Library, Archive
College founded 1923

Glassboro, N.J. 08028

(609) 445–6303
Contact: Special Collections Librarian

Mon.—Fri. 8:00am—4:00pm;
   1 eve. during academic year

No fee
Non-circulating, closed stacks, ID required

Published Guides: General guide.
Size of Collection: Approx. 14,000 vols., 60 manuscript drawers, plus pictures, maps.
Areas of Interest: New Jersey (except government documents, in a separate department). The collection includes some rare books, materials on genealogy, Quakers, Indians, and some United States history, especially war periods.
Women's Material: Includes minutes of Haddonfield Women's Meeting, 1725 to 1776, by Elizabeth Haddon and the Satterthwaite Genealogical Collection (working papers, letters, genealogies). The Howell papers include some materials by women in the family; the Miriam Hope diary, 5 vols., covers the period 1862 to 1871.

GLOUCESTER COUNTY HISTORICAL SOCIETY   NjWGHi

Library, Museum
Founded 1903

Museum: 58 North Broad Street
Library: 17 Hunter Street
Woodbury, N. J. 08096

(609) 845–4771
Contact: Librarian

Museum: Wed., Fri. 1:00pm—4:00pm
Library: Mon.—Fri. 1:00pm—4:00pm;
   Fri. 7:00pm—9:30pm
Last Sun. of month, 2:00pm–5:00pm

No fee

Size of Collection: Museum, 18 rooms; Library, 3 rooms.
Areas of Interest: Gloucester County and the general Delaware Valley area, including all South Jersey from the early seventeenth century to the present.
Women's Material: Approx. 10 percent of total. The museum collection includes: women's clothing—shoes, hats, dresses, gloves, fans, purses, wedding dresses, etc.; nineteenth-century kitchen equipment; sewing machines; personal items such as jewelry, combs, etc. The library has letters, account books, and manuscripts of Anna Blackwood Howell, and a diary of Rebecca Bee Turner.

See Hinding 11,207–11,212*

THE HAGLEY MUSEUM   DeWH

Museum (See also Eleutherian Mills Historical Library)
Founded 1957

P.O. Box 3630
Greenville
Wilmington, Del. 19807

(302) 658–2401
Contact: Curator of Collections

Tues.—Sat. 9:30am—4:30pm
Sun. 1:00pm—5:00pm

Museum fee: $2.50 adults; $1.00
students; $1.25 senior citizens

Published Guides: *Eleutherian Mills.*
Size of Collection: 15,000 items.
Areas of Interest: Technological artifacts relating both specifically to the site and to the larger concept of America's technological history; artifacts reflecting the social and cultural history of all strata of society which supported and implemented technological production in the Eleutherian Mills-Hagley area; specialized areas of interest inherent in the history of the Hagley Museum, i.e., the Du Pont Company and/or Du Pont family related materials.
Women's Material: Approx. 25 percent of total. Includes whitework embroidery done by the daughters of E. I. du Pont de Nemours (1771–1834) during the early nineteenth century and hooked rugs by unidentified makers. The collection has nineteenth-century artifacts as follows:

Appliances and Equipment
Clothing and Accessories
Furniture
Household Items

Paintings
Textiles
Toys and Amusements

HAHNEMANN UNIVERSITY—ARCHIVES AND HISTORY OF MEDICINE COLLECTIONS   PPHa

Health Sciences University
Founded 1848

245 North 15th Street
Mail Stop 912
Philadelphia, Pa. 19102

(215) 448–7811
Contact: Archivist/History of Medicine
Librarian

Mon.—Fri. 9:00am—5:00pm

No fee
No circulation;
photocopy service available

Size of Collection: ca. 1,500 vols., 250 lin. ft. archives.
Areas of Interest: Records and history of the institution, its constituents, and related organizations, 1848 to the present. The Archives have materials on the history of homeopathy and the history of medicine (especially) neuro-sciences, anatomy, Philadelphia; personal papers of faculty and alumni, and "Paracelsus."
Women's Material: The records of the Hahnemann Hospital Nurses' Alumnae Association, 1890 to ca. 1950 include minutes (1898–1949), financial records, membership lists, photographs, histories, and the newsletter (1946–1982); activity regarding PSNA nurses' registration, the eight-hour day, conventions, scholarships, etc. The collection also has some personal papers and memorabilia of nursing alumnae, including scrapbooks (1953–1956), material on the pioneer cardiac surgi-

cal nursing program, letters describing early experiences, etc. It has material from the Hahnemann Hospital School of Nursing, 1890 to 1975, including yearbooks (1927–1974), catalogues, rosters, Dean's notebook (1942–1945), and memorabilia. Materials include biographical information on women homeopathic physicians and on constituent women's groups, i.e., the Hahnemann Hospital Association (1886 to present), Friends of the Likoff Cardiovascular Institute (formerly Mary Bailey Foundation), 1948 to present.

HARCUM JUNIOR COLLEGE   PBmH

College
Founded 1915

Montgomery and Morris Avenues   (215) 525–4100
Bryn Mawr, Pa. 19010   Contact: President of the college

Mon.—Fri. 9:00am—5:00pm   No fee
By appointment

Size of Collection: NA
Areas of Interest: Records of the women's College founded by Edith Harcum.
Women's Material: Records of the College and materials on Edith Harcum.

HAVERFORD COLLEGE LIBRARY—QUAKER COLLECTION   PHC

Library
College founded 1833, Collection founded 1867

Haverford, Pa. 19041   (215) 896–1161
                                       Contact: Curator

Mon.—Fri. 9:00am—4:30pm, acad. yr.   No fee
Mon.—Fri. 9:00am—4:00pm, summer
Closed 12:30pm—1:30pm

Published Guides: *The Quaker Collection of the Haverford College Library.*
Size of Collection: 25,000 bound vols., 248,000 manuscripts.
Areas of Interest: The Religious Society of Friends in Britain and America, especially Philadelphia, seventeenth century to the present. The Collection has materials on the Society as a whole and individuals.
Women's Material: Includes manuscript journals and diaries, 1683 to 1954; Minutes of women's meetings, 1680 to the present. The Collection has some art works by Cecilia Beaux, Francoise André, and Amelia Opie, and a bust of Elizabeth Fry.

See Hinding 14,836–14,858

HISTORICAL SOCIETY OF DELAWARE   DeHi

Library
Founded 1864

505 Market Street Mall
Wilmington, Del. 19801

(302) 655–7161
Contact: Director of Library

Mon. 1:00pm—9:00pm
Tues.—Fri. 9:00am—5:00pm

No fee
Some collections restricted

Published Guides: To manuscript books.
Size of Collection: 1½ million items (manuscripts).
Areas of Interest: Material relating to the State of Delaware and its people from the time of settlement to the present.
Women's Material: 15 percent of total. Includes collections of various organizations run by women for social, political, and charitable reasons. The library also has a collection of suffrage-related material and numerous bodies of correspondence, diaries, and miscellaneous documents generated by women on both important and everyday matters, spanning two centuries. The Society has nineteenth- and twentieth-century books and periodicals in the following areas:

Behavior	Literature
Domestic Activity	Minorities and Ethnicity
Education	Religion
Feminism and Reform	Social Life
Law	

It has nineteenth- and twentieth-century manuscripts in the following areas:

Art, Architecture, Decorative Arts	Law
Behavior	Literature
Charities	Minorities and Ethnicity
Domestic Activity	Religion
Education	Science
Feminism and Reform	Social Life

See Hinding 2,034–2,063*

HISTORICAL SOCIETY OF THE EASTERN PENNSYLVANIA CONFERENCE OF THE UNITED METHODIST CHURCH   PPMHi

Saint George's Church, Library, Archive, Museum
Founded 1769

326 New Street
Philadelphia, Pa. 19106

(215) 925–7788
Contact: Administrator

Tues.—Fri. 10:00am—3:00pm

No fee
Archive searches by appointment

Size of Collection: 1 room library, 2 room museum.
Areas of Interest: The library contains many books on Methodism. The museum contains Methodist memorabilia and memorabilia of the founding of the Church.
Women's Material: Portrait of Anna Jarvis, who attended Saint George's Church and was the founder of Mother's Day.

Library, Archive, Museum
Founded 1824

1300 Locust Street
Philadelphia, Pa. 19107

(215) 732–6200
Contact: Librarian, Chief of Manuscripts, Curator of Galleries

Libraries: Mon. 1:00pm—9:00pm;
   Tues.—Fri. 9:00am—5:00pm
Galleries: Tues.—Sat. 9:00am—5:00pm

Galleries no fee
Libraries $1.00/day for non-members
Some restrictions

Published Guides: *Afro-Americana, 1553–1906; Paintings and Miniatures at the Historical Society of Pennsylvania; Guide to the Manuscript Collections,* 2d ed., 3d ed. in preparation.

Size of Collection: 200,000 books, 200,000 pamphlets, 14 million manuscripts, 650 paintings, etc.

Areas of Interest: Human activity in Pennsylvania generally and in the Delaware Valley in particular, although the book and manuscript collections are much more comprehensive than suggested by that policy. The history of English-speaking America and England are well documented for the eighteenth century. The collections become increasingly regional and local in the nineteenth and twentieth centuries.

Women's Material: 20 percent of total. Includes a number of large collections reflecting the political life of women: the archives of the League of Women Voters, both the state organization and the Philadelphia office; the councilmanic papers of Constance H. Dallas; and the papers of women's rights advocate Caroline Katzenstein, 1910 to 1963. The philanthropic and social concerns of women are represented in such collections as: the Society of the Relief of Indigent Widows and Single Women, 1823 to 1862; the papers of the House of Refuge, 1826 to 1910 and of the Magdalen Society, 1800 to 1855; and of the American Association of University Women, Philadelphia office. Papers of the Women's Dental Association and a number of other organizations document the professional life of women, as do the large collections of pamphlets and annual reports in the library. Individual women whose personal papers or writings may be found at the Society include: Elizabeth Drinker, Sarah Logan Fisher, Grace Galloway, Florence Bayard Kane, Deborah Logan, Hannah Penn, and many others. Personal and business papers of most of the women represented in the collections are to be found among the papers of the families of which they were a part. The society holds seventeenth-, eighteenth-, nineteenth-, and twentieth-century printed, handwritten, and some audio/visual material in the following areas:

Art, Architecture, Decorative Arts	Minorities and Ethnicity
Behavior	Performing Arts
Charities	Religion
Domestic Activity	Sciences
Education	Sex
Feminism and Reform	Social Life
Law	Statistics
Literature	Work
Medicine	

The collection also includes a number of drawings and paintings and numerous photographs and prints.

By a cooperative agreement with the Library Company of Philadelphia, many of the

Society's rare books are housed at the Library Company and the Library Company manuscripts are at the Society.

See Hinding 14,945–15,122*

HOLY CHILD ARCHIVES—AMERICAN PROVINCE   PRosHC

Roman Catholic Religious Congregation Archive (See also Rosemont College and Rosemont College—Institute of Studies on the Society of the Holy Child Jesus) Order founded 1846

1341 Montgomery Avenue
Rosemont, Pa. 19010

Mon.—Fri. 9:00am—4:00pm

(215) 527–3486
Contact: Archivist

No fee
Open to qualified researchers

Size of Collection: NA
Areas of Interest: Records of the American Province of the Sisters of the Holy Child Jesus, 1846 to the present. Materials include House diaries of closed Houses, records of the Provincial office, reports of Chapters and Convocations, and letters from the General Superior in Rome, and from the American Provincials. The collection also has correspondence of Cornelia Connelly, founder of the order, and books and articles written by members of the congregation.
Women's Material: Approx. 90 percent of total. See above. The Archives have a collection of oral history tapes which record many interviews of early sisters.

See Hinding 15,265

HOLY FAMILY COLLEGE   PPHFC

College Archive (See also Immaculate Conception of the Blessed Virgin Mary Province Archives)
College founded 1954, Archives founded 1972

Grant and Frankford Avenues
Philadelphia, Pa. 19114

Mon.—Fri. 9:00am—2:30pm

(215) 637–6262
Contact: Archivist

No fee
Some personnel records restricted

Published Guides: *Guide to Nazareth Literature 1873–1973.*
Size of Collection: 800 cu. ft.
Areas of Interest: Annals, chronicles, records, faculty papers, tape recordings, outlines of courses, and bulletins of faculty members. The Frank Hartman Collection Series comprises various periodicals dealing with nuclear energy, radiation, and its uses in medicine and radioactive elements. The archive also has the Dr. Leon Kolankiewicz Collection Series on Polish heritage, the Stephen Sokolowski Collection Series on journalism, and the John A. Wojciechowicz Collection Series on Polish arts clubs.
Women's Material: 85 percent of total. Records of Holy Family College, founded and administered by and for women. The archive has local history collections and information on Virginia Knauer, Marie Curie-Sklodowski, Marion Coleman and Helena Paderewska. The collection includes theses of members of the Order on the following topics:

Art, Architecture, Decorative Arts
Domestic Activity
Education
Feminism and Reform
Literature

Medicine
Minorities and Ethnicity
Performing Arts
Religion
Sciences

IMMACULATE CONCEPTION OF THE BLESSED VIRGIN MARY PROVINCE ARCHIVES   PPCSFN

Roman Catholic Religious Congregation Archive (See also Holy Family College)
Order established in Philadelphia 1892

Grant and Frankford Avenues
Philadelphia, Pa. 19114

(215) 637–6464
Contact: Archivist

Mon.—Fri. 9:00am—2:30pm

No fee
Some personnel records restricted

Published Guides: *Guide to Nazareth Literature 1873–1973.*
Size of Collection: 834.5 cu. ft., 875 books.
Areas of Interest: Include records, literary works, and fine arts by members of
the Congregation; historical collections of general and local interest; and records
of the Province: books, pamphlets, magazine articles, published and unpublished
theses, research papers, essays, projects, fine arts, musical compositions, addresses,
plays, poems, and recordings. The archive has convent chronicles, parish anniver-
sary books and publications of the various apostolates, school papers, literary news,
bulletins, leaflets, and newspaper articles.
Women's Material: 98 percent of total. Covers the founding and history of the
Congregation of the Sisters of the Holy Family of Nazareth and of the Immaculate
Conception of the Blessed Virgin Mary Province of the sisters. Biographical material
covers the founder, and includes works of the members of the Congregation and
persons closely related to it. Geographical information is available on convents and
apostolates where the sisters minister and institutions with which they are connected.
The collection has theses by members of the Order on the following topics:

Art, Architecture, Decorative Arts
Behavior
Education
Feminism and Reform
History
Law

Literature
Minorities and Ethnicity
Performing Arts
Religion
Sciences
Work

See Hinding 15,179–15,181*

INA ARCHIVES   PPINA

Insurance Company Archive
Founded 1792

Insurance Company of North America
1600 Arch Street
Philadelphia, Pa. 19101

(215) 241–3293
Contact: Archivist/Historian

Mon.—Fri. 8:00am—5:00pm No fee
By appointment

Published Guides: Brochures and published history.

Size of Collection: 1,600 cu. ft., plus audio and video tape, 360 rolls microfilm, memorabilia.

Areas of Interest: Records of continuing value generated and used by the Insurance Company of North America since 1792 and INA companies since 1904 during the course of business. These records document corporate structure programs, policies, decisions, product lines, and communications.

Women's Material: Includes bulletins to key management, news releases, and company publications indexed for women from 1977, also material printed in the 1940s. The Archive has stockholder lists from 1792, eighteenth- and nineteenth-century day books (blotters), and records of owners of perpetual fire insurance, 1841 to 1957, all of which include names of women.

See Hinding 15,123

INDEPENDENCE NATIONAL HISTORICAL PARK   PPINHP

Museum
Founded 1948

313 Walnut Street
Philadelphia, Pa. 19106

(215) 597–7086
Contact: Chief Curator

Daily 9:00am—5:00pm
Independence Hall, Bishop White
    House, Todd House by guided tour
    only

No fee

Published Guides: *Treasures of Independence; Faces of Independence: Portrait Gallery Guidebook; The Branded Windsor Furniture of Independence National Historical Park.*

Size of Collection: 20,000 items.

Areas of Interest: The Park's themes are the American Revolution, Benjamin Franklin, and Philadelphia—Capital City. The collection concentrates on items that were or would have been used in a Park building during the period 1774 to 1800.

Women's Material: The most significant materials are those used to recreate accurate households in several of the Park's historic homes (Todd House, Bishop White House). Kitchens, parlors, dining rooms, and bed chambers have all been reassembled, providing glimpses into the daily lives of the prominent and wealthy (Mrs. William White), the efficient housekeeper for the White family (Mrs. Boggs), the young Quaker mother and wife (Dolley Todd, later Dolley Madison), and a teenager (Annie Payne). Furnishing Plans support the selection and use of specific items for these refurnished houses. Also included in both homes are many eighteenth- and early nineteenth-century books that relate to the proper role to be played by women—cookbooks, books on manners, etc.

Organization to Train Women Volunteers and Demonstrate, through Individual
 Projects, the Effectiveness of Trained Volunteers
Founded 1912

Free Quaker Meeting House	(215) 923–6777
5th and Arch Streets	Contact: President
Philadelphia, Pa. 19106	
June, July, Aug.: Tues.—Sun.	No fee

Size of Collection: NA

Areas of Interest: Women's participation in volunteer, social service activities. The
League also administers a museum.

Women's Material: Records of Junior League activities, 1912 to the present, pertain
to Philadelphia area volunteering and formation of social services. The material
includes minutes, handbooks, training manuals, and news sheets. The museum
collection includes an early Quaker wedding dress and a pattern for the star made
by Betsy Ross for the first United States flag.

LA SALLE COLLEGE ART MUSEUM PPLas

College Art Museum
Founded 1975

20th Street and Olney Avenue	(215) 951–1221
Philadelphia, Pa. 19141	Contact: Curator
Mon.—Fri. 11:00am—3:00pm;	No fee
Sun. 2:00pm—4:00pm	

Published Guides: Typewritten guide sheets in galleries.

Size of Collection: NA

Areas of Interest: Paintings, old master drawings, prints, sculpture, decorative
arts, rare books, and bibles from the fifteenth to the twentieth century, Europe and
America.

Women's Material: Works of art by women artists; prints, paintings, drawings, and
sculpture portraying women.

LEMON HILL MANSION PPLH

Museum
Founded—NA

East River and Sedgeley Drives	(215) 232–4337
Philadelphia, Pa. 19130	Contact: Antiquarian
Wed.—Sun. 10:00am—4:00pm	Fee: $1.00 adults; $.50 children

Size of Collection: NA

Areas of Interest: Interpretation of 1799 to 1800 house built by Henry Pratt. The
house is administered by the Colonial Dames of America.

Women's Material: The furnishings and building illustrate the life of an upper-
class family of the early nineteenth century.

LIBRARY COMPANY OF PHILADELPHIA   PPL

Library
Founded 1731

1314 Locust Street	(215) 546–3181/2465
Philadelphia, Pa. 19107	Contact: Reference Staff
Mon.—Fri. 9:00am—4:45pm	No fee

Published Guides: *Afro-Americana 1553–1906, The Library of James Logan.* Manuscript collection will be included in 3d ed. of *Guide to the Historical Society of Pennsylvania Collections* (forthcoming). Guides to holdings of American education, natural history, philanthropy, and agriculture to be published in near future.
Size of Collection: 450,000 items.

Areas of Interest: Historic collection of Anglo-American civilization, 1690 to 1870 has particular strength in: practical and applied science and mechanics; American medicine to 1820; art and architecture to 1860; voyages and travels; Afro-American history to 1906; prints, drawings, and photography concentrating on the city of Philadelphia and environs; women's history in America to 1880; agriculture and natural history to 1860; philanthropy and education in America before 1860. The library also has literature and manuscripts relating to the Company's institutional history or collections of association copies and early American bibliophiles.

Women's Material: 35 percent of total. Major manuscript collections include: poets Hannah Griffitts (1727–1817) and Susanna Wright (1697–1784) and author and translator Elizabeth Graeme Ferguson (1737–1801). The Rush Family Papers include Julia Stockton Rush (1759–1848), Anne Emily Rush (1779–1850), and Mary Stockton. The collections of printed and manuscript materials include: poet Phillis Wheatley (ca. 1753–1784), critic and foreign correspondent Anne Hampton Brewster (1819–1892), the library of Mary Rebecca Darby Smith (1814–1886), and the ornithological collection of Louise Elkins Sinkler (1890–1977). Subject collections of printed women's historical material include: philanthropic, reform, and educational groups to 1890; anti-slavery groups to 1860; early American women printers; early women's rights to 1880; and printed books, scrapbooks, commonplace, and autograph books owned by prominent Philadelphia area women of the eighteenth and nineteenth centuries. The collection includes printed and handwritten materials from the seventeenth through nineteenth centuries in the following areas:

Art, Architecture, Decorative Arts	Minorities and Ethnicity
Behavior	Performing Arts
Charities	Religion
Domestic Activity	Sciences
Education	Sex
Feminism and Reform	Social Life
Law	Statistics
Literature	Work
Medicine	

The Library Company also has eighteenth- through twentieth-century artifacts as follows:

Drawings	Prints
Household Items	Sculpture
Paintings	Textiles
Photographs	Toys and Amusements

By a cooperative agreement with the Historical Society of Pennsylvania, the Library

Company's manuscripts are housed at the Historical Society and many of the Historical Society's rare books are at the Library Company.

LUTHERAN ARCHIVES CENTER AT PHILADELPHIA PPLT

Archive
Founded 1748

7301 Germantown Avenue
Philadelphia, Pa. 19119

Mon.—Fri. 9:30am—1:30pm

(215) 248–4616, Ext. 34
Contact: Curator

Fee: $5.00

Size of Collection: 700 ft.
Areas of Interest: Records of Lutheran congregations, synods, institutions, and organizations in Eastern Pennsylvania, New Jersey, upper New York, and relating to Slovak Lutherans throughout the country, 1700 to the present.
Women's Material: 23 percent of total. Includes files of the Women's Missionary Society of the Ministerium of Pennsylvania and successor organizations, 1880s to the present (minutes, publications, correspondence, etc.). The Archives also have files of the Philadelphia Seminary Women's Auxiliary, 1939 to the present, and materials relating to women's organizations within the Lutheran congregation.

EBENEZER MAXWELL MANSION, INC. PPMM

Historic House Museum
Founded 1965

200 West Tulpehocken Street
Philadelphia, Pa. 19144

Wed., Sat. 11:00am—4:00pm;
    Sun. 1:00pm—5:00pm
By appointment with director

(215) 438–1861
Contact: Director

Fee: $1.00

Size of Collection: NA
Areas of Interest: The collection focuses on items needed to interpret the lifestyle of an average mid-nineteenth-century middle-class family.
Women's Material: The period rooms of the house form an artifact that illustrates the setting for the life of a middle-class woman of the mid-nineteenth century. A few items, such as costumes and handiwork are directly relevant.

MEDICAL COLLEGE OF PENNSYLVANIA, ARCHIVES AND SPECIAL COLLECTIONS ON WOMEN IN MEDICINE PPMCP

Archive
Founded 1850 as the Female Medical College of Pennsylvania

3300 Henry Avenue
Philadelphia, Pa. 19144
Mon.—Fri. 8:00am—4:00pm

(215) 842–7124
Contact: Director
No fee
No loans, limited photocopying

Published Guides: *Guide to Archives and Special Collections; Catalogue to the Oral History Collection.*

Size of Collection: 700 lin. ft.

Areas of Interest: Non-current records of the first and only extant college organized exclusively for the education of women physicians. The collection includes the personal and business papers of women physicians and women's medical organizations and connected individuals and organizations. The scope is international, 1840s to the present, with the heaviest concentration in the United States.

Women's Material: 100 percent of total (see above). Includes student theses from the nineteenth century; records of now-extinct women's hospitals and medical schools; personal correspondence of women physicians, especially in Philadelphia and Pennsylvania; a book collection on women in medicine; and a photograph collection. The Archives have nineteenth- and twentieth-century printed, hand-written, and audio/visual materials in the following areas:

Art, Architecture, Decorative Arts	Minorities and Ethnicity
Behavior	Performing Arts
Charities	Religion
Domestic Activity	Sciences
Education	Sex
Feminism and Reform	Social Life
Law	Statistics
Literature	Technology
Medicine	Work

The College also has nineteenth- and twentieth-century artifacts:

Appliances and Equipment	Paintings
Clothing and Accessories	Photographs
Drawings	Scientific Apparatus
Medical Instruments	Sculpture
Oriental Artifacts	Toys and Amusements

See Hinding 15,125–15,145*

MERCER MUSEUM OF THE BUCKS COUNTY HISTORICAL SOCIETY
PDoBHi

Museum
Founded 1916

Pine and Green Streets
Doylestown, Pa. 18901

(215) 345–0210
Contact: Registrar, Assistant Curator

Mon.—Sat. 10:00am—5:00pm;
   Sun. 1:00pm—5:00pm
Museum closed Jan. & Feb.
Study collections by appointment

Fee: $2.00 Adults; $1.00 Students; $1.50
   Senior Citizens

Published Guides: *Pennsylvania Pottery—Tools and Processes; Pennsylvania Butter—Tools and Processes; Handmade Hats—Tools and Processes; Tools and Trades of America's Past.*

Size of Collection: 60,000 objects.

Areas of Interest: A comprehensive collection of tools, machines, and end products of the American pre-industrial era. The collection includes tools of farmers, craftsmen, tradesmen, artisans, housewives, lawyers, doctors, etc. The emphasis is on the vernacular rather than academic style. Preference is given to local objects and those which date to the "pre-steam" era of technology.

Women's Material: 5–10 percent of total. The Museum has eighteenth- and nine-teenth-century artifacts as follows:

Appliances and Equipment	Paintings
Clothing and Accessories	Photographs
Furniture	Textiles
Household Items	Toys and Amusements
Musical Instruments	Victorian Home Art

MISSIONARY SERVANTS OF THE MOST BLESSED TRINITY   PPMSBT

Library, Archive, Research Office
Roman Catholic Religious Order established in Philadelphia 1931

3501 Solly Avenue
Philadelphia, Pa. 19136

Mon.—Fri. 9:00am—5:00pm

(215) 335–7500
Contact: Director of Research

No fee
Access restricted to research and archives offices

Size of Collection: NA

Areas of Interest: Records of the Motherhouse and Generalate of the Order in Philadelphia since 1931. The collection includes materials from missions, the Holy Redeemer Chinese School, Catholic Social Services, some parish ministries, the LaSalle Resource Center, and the Mother Boniface Center.

Women's Material: 90 percent of total. The research office has extensive materials on Mother Boniface Keasey, MSBT, co-founder of the community, including a geneo-gram, slide presentations, photographs, letters, and oral history tapes. The archive has administrative accounts, the history of mission activities, and current publica-tions of the communications office and the LaSalle Resource Center. The collection has twentieth-century printed, machine-readable, and some audio/visual material in the following areas:

Education	Statistics
Religion	Work

It also has a large number of photographs and some textiles, all from the twentieth century.

See Hinding 15,146

MOORE COLLEGE OF ART   PPMo

Women's Art College—Library, Archive, Art & Costume Collections
Founded 1844 as the Philadelphia School of Design for Women

20th Street and the Parkway
Philadelphia, Pa. 19103

By appointment

(215) 568–4515
Contact: Library Director

No fee
Use of materials by permission
Non-circulating

Size of Collection: 33,000 books and periodicals; 73,000 slides; 1,000 art works; miscellaneous costumes, accessories, furniture, jewelry, household items.

Areas of Interest: Women artists and women in art, especially from the past, American and contemporary women artists, craftswomen, and women in the applied/ professional arts. The archives material focuses on late nineteenth-century women artists and art education. The general library and slide collection focuses on art, professional publications, and exhibition catalogues, especially on contemporary women artists (covering all fine arts, interior design, illustration, fashion design and illustration, photography, etc.). The Moore Art Collection consists primarily of late nineteenth- and twentieth-century American art. The Moore College of Art Alumnae Association Collection of Art consists primarily of alumnae works purchased by the Association.

Women's Material: The Archive holds original correspondence among the Sartain family (mid to late nineteenth-century Philadelphia artists and art educators), including letters from Emily Sartain describing her travels to Europe with Mary Cassatt and her growth as an artist. The College also has clippings, pamphlets, and photographs of the early history of Moore and the development of art education for women in Philadelphia, collected by Harriet Sartain and others. All the collections are significant in the history of women in art from the mid nineteenth century to the present, and especially in the history of Philadelphia area women artists and applied art professionals. The collection has nineteenth- and twentieth-century printed, handwritten, and some audio/visual materials on applied and professional arts; art, architecture, and decorative arts; education; and textile design and fashion. The College also has nineteenth- and twentieth-century art and artifacts as follows:

Clothing and Accessories
Drawings
Furniture
Household Items
Paintings

Photographs
Prints
Sculpture
Textiles

MUSEUM OF AMERICAN JEWISH HISTORY   PPMAJ

Library, Museum, Slide Library in progress
Founded 1976

55 North 5th Street
Philadelphia, Pa. 19106

(215) 932–3811
Contact: Curator

Mon.—Thurs. 10:00am—5:00pm;
   Sun. 12:00noon—5:00pm
Research by appointment

Fee: $1.50 Museum

Published Guides: Catalogues of past exhibitions: *Inaugural Exhibit; Philadelphia Sampler; The Role of the Jew in Forging the Nation; The Tallit as a Metaphor of Community; The American Jewish Experience 1654 to the Present.*

Size of Collection: Approx. 800 pieces.

Areas of Interest: The mandate is to preserve, document, and interpret Jewish participation in the growth and development of America from 1654 to the present. The geographical concentration includes North, Central, and South America.

Women's Material: 30 percent of total. The Rebecca Gratz Collection includes furniture, family portraits, clothing, jewelry, books, and personal items. The Museum also has the trousseau of Eleanor Solis-Cohen (1886–1981) and a variety of nineteenth-century portraits. The Museum has nineteenth-century printed materials on art, architecture, decorative arts, and literature. It also has nineteenth- and twentieth-century artifacts as follows:

Clothing and Accessories	Photographs
Furniture	Religious Artifacts
Paintings	Textiles

MUSEUM OF THE PHILADELPHIA CIVIC CENTER PPComm-M

Museum
Founded 1894

34th Street and Civic Center Boulevard
Philadelphia, Pa. 19104

(215) 823–7204
Contact: Curator of Education

Museum: Tues.—Sat. 9:00am—5:00pm;
Sun. 1:00pm—5:00pm
Serious scholars by appointment:
Mon.—Fri. 9:00am—5:00pm

No fee

Published Guides: Catalogues of African and musical instrument collections.
Size of Collection: Approx. 10,000 objects.
Areas of Interest: The collection was acquired from several international expositions at the turn of the century. It includes contemporaneous ethnographic materials from Asia, Africa, and Latin America.
Women's Material: African, Asian, and Latin American holdings include turn-of-the-century costumes, textiles, musical instruments, household utensils, decorative arts, appliances and equipment, ceremonial items, art work, and toys and amusements.

THE MUTUAL ASSURANCE COMPANY PPMA

Corporation Archive
Founded 1784

240 South 4th Street
Philadelphia, Pa. 19106

(215) 925–0609
Contact: Curator

By appointment

No fee
Some restrictions

Published Guides: *Catalogue of the Green Tree Collection The Architectural Surveys, 1784–1794.*
Size of Collection: NA
Areas of Interest: Items that pertain to the history of the Company, early insurance, and fire fighting in Philadelphia.
Women's Material: Policies and surveys issued by the Company on properties belonging to women. They do not differ from other policies and surveys and are not separately catalogued. The Company also has a portrait of J. Dickinson Sergeant, Esq., by Cecilia Beaux.

THE NATIONAL SOCIETY OF THE COLONIAL DAMES IN THE COMMONWEALTH OF PENNSYLVANIA   PPCD

Hereditary and Patriotic Society, Library, Historic House Museum
Founded 1891

Headquarters: 1630 Latimer Street Philadelphia, Pa. 19103	(215) 735–6737
Stenton: 18th and Courtland Streets Philadelphia, Pa. 19140	(215) 329–7312 Contact: President
Headquarters: Mon.—Fri. 9:00am— 5:00pm (closed Aug.)	No fee Some restrictions on Library
Stenton: Tues.—Sat. 1:00pm—5:00pm (closed Jan., Feb.)	Fee: $1.00

Size of Collection: 1,550 vols., 275 pamphlets.

Areas of Interest: The purpose of the Society is "to collect and preserve manuscripts, traditions, relics, and mementos of bygone days; to preserve and restore buildings connected with the early history of our country, to diffuse healthful and intelligent information concerning the past, to create a popular interest in our colonial history, to stimulate a spirit of true patriotism and a genuine love of country, and to impress upon the young the sacred obligation of honoring the memory of those heroic ancestors whose ability, valor, sufferings, and achievements are beyond all praise." The Society administers Stenton, an eighteenth-century house with grounds, has compiled biographies of colonial and pioneer women, and holds occasional symposia on colonial women.

Women's Material: 14 percent of library. The library holds books dealing with the history of colonial women, especially in Pennsylvania. Stenton is a fully furnished house museum with outbuildings illustrating eighteenth-century life, particularly of the Logan family. The library collection includes printed works on art, architecture, and decorative arts; domestic activity; and literature of the seventeenth and eighteenth centuries. Stenton includes a house, barn, and garden equipped with eighteenth- and nineteenth-century furnishings:

Farm Implements	Prints
Furniture	Spinning Equipment
Household Items	Textiles
Paintings	

NEUMANN COLLEGE   PAsN

College Archive (See also Our Lady of Angels Convent)
College founded 1965

Aston, Pa. 19014	(215) 459–0905 Contact: Archivist
Mon.—Fri. afternoon By appointment	No fee Some records restricted

Size of Collection: Approx. 110 boxes.

Areas of Interest: Records of the College.

Women's Material: Approx. 5 percent of total. Works by members of the Order of Saint Francis, dealing with the history of the order and education.

State Historic Preservation Office
Founded 1931 as the Historic Sites Commission

109 West State Street
Trenton, N.J. 08625

(609) 292–2028
Contact: Chief, OHP

Mon.—Fri. 8:30am—4:30pm

No fee

Published Guides: New Jersey and National Registers Directory (with supplements); *Annotated Bibliography of Cultural Resource Survey Reports Submitted to the New Jersey State Historic Preservation Office.*
Size of Collection: See below.
Areas of Interest: Include State and National Register nomination forms (description, significance, maps, photos) of over 750 individual properties and 100 historic districts; the New Jersey Historic Sites Inventory; and project-specific cultural resource surveys. Materials cover the entire state.
Women's Material: Properties associated with significant women ranging from the Elizabeth Cady Stanton House, Tenafly, to the Lotta Crabtree House, Mount Arlington, to the Dr. Sarah Clark House, Union Township, are on the State and National Registers. The records are not indexed according to themes.

See Hinding 11,185

NEW JERSEY STATE LIBRARY—ARCHIVES SECTION, BUREAU OF LAW, ARCHIVES, AND REFERENCE SERVICES   Nj

Archive
Founded 1897

CN 520
185 West State Street
Trenton, N. J. 08625

(609) 292–6260
Contact: Archivist I

Mon.—Fri. 8:30am—4:30pm

No fee

Size of Collection: NA
Areas of Interest: Official records of the state and colony of New Jersey, 1660s to the present.
Women's Material: Is scattered throughout most record groups: wills from the colonial period to 1900; tavern licenses, late 1700s to early 1800s; colonial deeds; laws and court records; pension claims of widows in military records; vital records, 1848–1878; recent governors' records.

See Hinding 11,186–11,206

OUR LADY OF ANGELS CONVENT (SISTERS OF SAINT FRANCIS OF PHILADELPHIA)   PAsOSF

Roman Catholic Religious Congregation Archive (See also Neumann College)
Founded 1855

Aston, Pa. 19014

(215) 459–4125
Contact: Archivist

By appointment

No fee
No circulation, some materials
restricted

Size of Collection: Approx. 310 lin. ft.

Areas of Interest: Records of four United States provinces and missions. The collection includes data on the institutions of the congregation and pictures, books, manuscripts, etc. Correspondence with church officials, etc., forms the major portion of the repository. There are some materials on Saint John Neumann.

Women's Material: Approx. 90 percent of total. Records of the congregation of women, administered by women, whose apostolates include educational and health facilities. The archive has data on the history of the congregation and the church in the United States, works on education, information about the hospitals of the congregation, and materials on social justice and social work. The collection has nineteenth- and twentieth-century printed, handwritten, machine-readable, and audio/visual materials in the following areas:

Art, Architecture, Decorative Arts
Biography
Diaries
Education
Literature

Minorities and Ethnicity
Newspaper Clippings
Religion
Sciences

It also has nineteenth- and twentieth-century artifacts as follows:

Clothing and Accessories
Paintings
Photographs

Prints
Religious Artifacts

See Hinding 14,719

PENNSBURY MANOR   PMoP

Historic Site (Reconstructed)
Original Manor built 1683 Historic Site established 1932

400 Pennsbury Memorial Road
Morrisville, Pa. 19067

(215) 946–0400
Contact: Administrator

Tues.—Sat. 9:00am—5:00pm;
   Sun. 12:00noon—5:00pm
Research by appointment

Fee: $1.50 adults; $1.00 senior citizens

Size of Collection: 750 original artifacts, 200 reproductions.

Areas of Interest: Early American (ca. 1700) and English decorative arts objects that assist in interpreting the life of the first governor and proprietor of Pennsylvania, William Penn. A small research library (approximately 250 volumes) contains secondary sources on social life and customs of the seventeenth century. Pennsbury is owned and operated by the Pennsylvania Historical and Museum Commission through the Bureau of Historic Sites in Harrisburg.

Women's Material: 8 percent of total. Illustrates the domestic role of women in the seventeenth century. The collection includes a large number of artifacts used by women in their role in the kitchen and household, including ceramic bowls, iron kettles, a butter churn, candle molds, etc., and a few textile pieces made by women as early decorative pieces. A documented period clothing collection portrays Quaker women's clothing, including chemises, petticoats, gowns, coifs, hoods, stuffers, pockets, etc. Two kitchens are totally equipped to interpret domestic life and cooking in the seventeenth and eighteenth centuries. Pennsbury has seventeenth-, eighteenth-, and nineteenth-century artifacts as follows:

Appliances and Equipment	Household Items
Clothing and Accessories	Paintings
Decorative Objects	Side Saddles
Furniture	Textiles

PENNSYLVANIA ACADEMY OF THE FINE ARTS PPPAFA

Art School, Library, Archive, Museum
Founded 1805

Broad and Cherry Streets
Philadelphia, Pa. 19102

(215) 972–7600
Contact: Curator

Tues.—Sat. 10:00am—5:00pm;
   Sun. 1:00pm—5:00pm

Fee: $1.50 adults; $1.00 senior citizens;
   $.50 students

Published Guides: *In This Academy,* others dealing with particular sections of the collection.
Size of Collection: Approx. 9,000 works of art, 7,000 vol. library, large archive.
Areas of Interest: Eighteenth- to twentieth-century American painting, sculpture, and graphic arts. The Academy has one of the most important collections of American art in the country.
Women's Material: Approx. 20 percent of total. Works by women artists have always been collected and the Academy holds examples of many of the most significant of them. The archive has unique and original documents relating to women Academy students, as well as research material on works in the collection by women artists. The library has an extensive clipping file on women artists.

PENNSYLVANIA HOSPITAL—LIBRARY PPPH

Hospital Library, Archive
Hospital founded 1752, Archive founded 1976

8th and Spruce Streets
Philadelphia, Pa. 19107

(215) 829–3998
Contact: Librarian/Archivist

Mon.—Fri. 8:30am—5:00pm

No fee
Admission by advance phone or written permission

Size of Collection: Approx. 1,000 lin. ft.
Areas of Interest: Materials related to health and/or Pennsylvania Hospital.
Women's Material: Approx. 20 percent of total. Includes general records of Pennsylvania Hospital patients. The archive also has records of the Maternity Hospital, the Pennsylvania Hospital Training School for Nurses, the Philadelphia Lying-In Charity Hospital, and the Preston Retreat, a lying-in hospital for working class women.

See Hinding 15,148–15,151

PERELMAN ANTIQUE TOY MUSEUM   PPPT

Museum
Founded 1969

270 South 2nd Street   (215) 922–1070
Philadelphia, Pa. 19106   Contact: Curator

Mon.—Sat. 9:30am—5:00pm;   Fee: $1.00 adults; $.55 children
   Sun. 9:30am—4:00pm

Published Guides: Brochure.
Size of Collection: 4,000 toys.
Areas of Interest: Toys made between 1850 and 1920, mainly in the United States.
Women's Material: 3 percent of total. Includes a doll collection of approximately 120 items.

PHILADELPHIA COLLEGE OF ART—LIBRARY   PAI

Art College Library
College founded as Pennsylvania Museum and School of Industrial Art 1876

Broad and Spruce Streets   (215) 893–3127
Philadelphia, Pa. 19102   Contact: Library Director

Mon.—Fri. 9:00am—5:00pm with vari-   No fee
   ation   Borrowing restricted

Size of Collection: NA
Areas of Interest: The arts, with some emphasis on the contemporary and on works by and about the college faculty, alumni, students, etc.
Women's Material: Includes some original art works, books, and exhibitions announcements, etc. by or about women associated with the College. The College has a large slide library illustrating works by women faculty currently or formerly in the painting, photography, and sculpture departments, as well as by local illustrators and by craftswomen nationwide. The collection also includes scenes of Turkish village life photographed by anthropologist Ayse Daher and depicting costumes, cooking, utensils, and agriculture.

PHILADELPHIA COLLEGE OF TEXTILES AND SCIENCE—GOLDIE PALEY DESIGN CENTER   PPPCT-P

Archive, Gallery
Founded 1978

4200 Henry Avenue   (215) 951–2860
Philadelphia, Pa. 19144   Contact: Director

Tues.—Sat. 10:00am—4:00pm   No fee

Size of Collection: Over 200,000 items.
Areas of Interest: A study collection of over 400,000 fabric samples representing the actual work and the design models from many European and American textile mills is used primarily as a fabric library. The historical collection contains pieces

from before the fourth century to the present. Geographically, they represent the world.

Women's Material: Includes costumes made and worn by women; quilts and coverlets made and used by women; lace, crotchet, needlepoint, and embroidery made and used by women, and some appliances and pieces of equipment.

PHILADELPHIA COLLEGE OF TEXTILES AND SCIENCE—PASTORE LIBRARY   PPPCT-PL

Library
Founded 1884 as part of Pennsylvania Museum of Art

School House Lane and Henry Avenue   (215) 951–2847
Philadelphia, Pa. 19144   Contact: Director

Mon.—Thurs. 8:30am—10:00pm; Fri.   No fee
  8:30am—7:00pm; Sat. 10:00am—   Open to public for reference
  5:00pm; Sun. 12:00noon—8:00pm

Published Guides: Various pathfinders on textile subjects.
Size of Collection: 70,000 items.
Areas of Interest: Primarily an undergraduate instructional collection with research depth in business and textiles. Special collections emphasize the textiles industry in Philadelphia in the nineteenth and twentieth centuries.
Women's Material: Includes a fashion and costume design collection, information on twentieth-century women in the trade union movement (UMI), and some early works by women on textiles and apparel. The Library has nineteenth- and twentieth-century materials in the following areas:

Art, Architecture, Decorative Arts   Technology
Behavior   Work

It also has photographs and textiles.

THE PHILADELPHIA CONTRIBUTIONSHIP   PPPC

Corporate Collection—Active Insurance Company
Founded 1752

212 South 4th Street   (215) 627–1752
Philadelphia, Pa. 19106   Contact: Curator/Archivist

Mon.—Fri. 10:00am—3:00pm   No fee
                                        Open to qualified researchers by
                                        appointment

Size of Collection: NA
Areas of Interest: Records and memorabilia of the company.
Women's Material: Surveys and policies on properties owned by women from the eighteenth, nineteenth, and twentieth centuries. The materials do not differ from those on properties held by men, and are not catalogued separately. The collection also includes a waterman's armband made by Hester Bateman in London in 1776, and photographs showing female housekeepers and office workers in the early to mid-twentieth century.

PHILADELPHIA HISTORICAL COMMISSION   PPHC

Library, Archive, Architectural Research/Historical Preservation
Founded 1955

1313 City Hall Annex
Philadelphia, Pa. 19107

(215) 686–4543/4583
Contact: Research Historian

Mon.—Fri. 8:30am—5:00pm

No fee
No circulation

Size of Collection: 1,500 vols., 20 map drawers, 90 file drawers.

Areas of Interest: Any material relating to the history of Philadelphia, especially its architectural heritage, including chains of titles, copies of building permits, newspaper clippings, histories, photographs, and any other item pertaining to a particular building, architect, or neighborhood.

Women's Material: Is included in some records, particularly chains of titles, but is not indexed separately. Most of the collection was assembled between 1956 and 1975 by women, especially Margaret Tinkcom, co-author of *Historic Germantown* and author of numerous articles, Beatrice Kirkbride, and Marjorie Mauer. Notable items within the collection include historic structure reports by Penelope H. Batcheler and archaeological reports by Barbara Liggett.

PHILADELPHIA JEWISH ARCHIVES CENTER   PPJA

Archive
Founded 1972

625 Walnut Street
Philadelphia, Pa. 19106

(215) 923–2729
Contact: Archivist

Mon.—Fri. 8:00am—4:00pm;
   7:30am—3:00pm, summer

No fee
Some collections restricted

Published Guides: *A Guide to the Philadelphia Jewish Archives Center;* twice yearly newsletter.

Size of Collection: NA

Areas of Interest: Depository for records of the Philadelphia Jewish community, any dates, including official records, personal papers, manuscripts, pictorial records, and artifacts.

Women's Material: Includes records of the Hebrew Sunday School Society, 1838 to the present; the Association for Jewish Children, 1855 to 1974; the Friends of the Deaf, 1936 to 1973; the Neighborhood Centre, ca. 1901 to 1967; and the Rebecca Gratz Club, 1909 to the 1950s. Papers include some of individual women. The Center has nineteenth- and twentieth-century printed and handwritten materials in the following areas:

Art, Architecture, Decorative Arts
Charities
Education
Jewish History

Literature
Minorities and Ethnicity
Religion

See Hinding 15,153–15,166

PHILADELPHIA MARITIME MUSEUM   PPPMM

Museum
Founded 1961

321 Chestnut Street
Philadelphia, Pa. 19106

(215) 925–5439
Contact: Librarian; Assistant Curator/
    Registrar

Mon.—Sat. 10:00am—5:00pm;
    Sun. 1:00pm—5:00pm

Fee: $1.00 adults; $.50 children

Size of Collection: 5,000 items.
Areas of Interest: The Museum collects, preserves, and interprets the maritime heritage of the Bay and River Delaware. All of the ports, naval activities, social and economic institutions and industries related to this waterway are the concern of the Museum. It covers the seventeenth century to the present.
Women's Material: Less than 1 percent of total. Includes journals and records of women accompanying their husbands on voyages.

See Hinding 15,167–15,168

PHILADELPHIA MUSEUM OF ART   PPPM

Museum with Library and Archive
Founded 1876

Benjamin Franklin Parkway at 25th Street
Mailing Address: Box 7646
Philadelphia, Pa. 19101

(215) 763–8100
Contact: Office of the Director; Public
    Relations

Tues.—Sun. 10:00am—5:00pm
Some galleries closed Tues.
Material not on view may be seen by
    appointment.

Fee: $2.50 adults; $1.25 students and
    senior citizens
Some restrictions on library use

Published Guides: *Guide, Treasures of the Philadelphia Museum,* other specialized publications on aspects of the collection.
Size of Collection: Over 500,000 objects.
Areas of Interest: Primary and secondary materials in the following curatorial departments: American Art; Costume and Textiles; European Decorative Arts After 1700; European Painting Before 1900; Far Eastern Art; Indian Art; Kienbusch Collection of Armor and Arms; Mediaeval and Renaissance Decorative Arts; Prints, Drawings, and Photographs; and Twentieth-Century Art. The dates covered by the collection are approximately 500 A.D. to the present. (Ancient, Tribal, and American Indian art are generally excluded, by an agreement with the University Museum.)
Women's Material: The department of Costumes and Textiles primarily contains material created for or by women. Mary Cassatt and Georgia O'Keeffe are well represented and the Museum collects work of many twentieth-century women artists. Patrons have included Mrs. Bloomfield Moore, whose gifts of thousands of objects built the early decorative arts collections. Mrs. Wilstach donated funds in memory of her husband for the acquisition of paintings that turned the direction of the Museum's growth from exclusive concentration on decorative and industrial arts to the inclusion of the fine arts. The Museum's library and archive have material

recording the history of women's activities in the Museum and in the Philadelphia area. In particular, the collection includes records of the Museum's Women's Committee, founded in 1883. The Museum also administers three Park Houses which illustrate the environment of certain eighteenth-century women: Mount Pleasant (1761), Cedar Grove (1721), and Solitude (1785). The library and archive have printed materials in the following areas:

Art, Architecture, Decorative Arts	Domestic Activity
Behavior	Education
Charities	

The Museum has art and artifacts as follows:

Appliances and Equipment	Photographs
Clothing and Accessories	Prints
Drawings	Religious Artifacts
Furniture	Sculpture
Household Items	Textiles
Paintings	

PHILADELPHIA ORCHESTRA ASSOCIATION   PPO

Orchestra, Archive (See also The Volunteers for the Philadelphia Orchestra)
Founded 1900

1420 Locust Street	(215) 893–1900
Philadelphia, Pa. 19102	Contact: Manager
Mon.—Fri. 9:00am—5:00pm	No fee

Size of Collection: NA
Areas of Interest: Holds records of the Philadelphia Orchestra.
Women's Material: Files include records of women employed as full-time musicians with the Philadelphia Orchestra since its inception in 1900.

PHILADELPHIA WOMEN'S COALITION—WOMENS WAY   PPWW

Women's Fund Raising Organization
Founded 1976

1501 Cherry Street	(215) 988–0227
Philadelphia, Pa. 19102	Contact: Executive Director
Mon.—Fri. 9:00am—5:00pm	No fee

Size of Collection: NA
Areas of Interest: Fund-raising coalition of organizations providing innovative, non-traditional services for Philadelphia area women.
Women's Material: 100 percent of total. Records of the organization.

Club for Professional Women Artists
Founded 1897

247 South Camac Street
Philadelphia, Pa. 19107

By appointment

(215) 545–9324
Contact: Archivist

No fee
No loans

Size of Collection: NA
Areas of Interest: Professional women artists, Club records.
Women's Material: Records of the Club and extensive information on Delaware Valley women artists from 1897 to the present.

PRESBYTERIAN HISTORICAL SOCIETY   PPPrHi

Library, Archive, Museum
Founded 1852

425 Lombard Street
Philadelphia, Pa. 19147

Mon.—Fri. 9:00am—5:00pm

(215) 627–1852
Contact: Research Historian

No fee
Some restrictions

Size of Collection: 200,000 titles in library, 13 million manuscripts.
Areas of Interest: All record forms (manuscript, print, non-print, realia) presenting information regarding American Presbyterian and Reformed church life, including their overseas mission operations. The collection covers the seventeenth to the twentieth centuries in the United States and abroad.
Women's Material: Includes records of the Woman's Foreign Missionary Society, Philadelphia; records pertinent to Philadelphia Presbyterian congregations' women's missionary, benevolent, and educational societies; Philadelphia presbyterial (women) and Presbytery level mission societies; Presbyterian retirement homes for women in Philadelphia; and biographical data regarding Philadelphia women who have served American Presbyterian churches as clergy or missionaries or prominent laypersons. The same types of information are available for Presbyterian women for counties contiguous to Philadelphia, for southern New Jersey, and the state of Delaware. The collection includes eighteenth-, nineteenth-, and twentieth-century printed and handwritten materials in the following areas:

Art, Architecture, Decorative Arts	Literature
Behavior	Medicine
Charities	Religion
Education	Work
Feminism and Reform	

The Society also has eighteenth-, nineteenth-, and twentieth-century artifacts:

Clothing and Accessories	Prints
Furniture	Religious Artifacts
Paintings	Textiles
Photographs	

See Hinding 15,171–15,176

PRINCETON UNIVERSITY—ART MUSEUM   NjP-M

Museum
Museum founded 1882

Princeton, N.J. 08544

(609) 452–3788
Contact: Curator of Collections

Tues.—Sat. 10:00am—4:00pm
Sun. 1:00pm—5:00pm academic year
Sun. 2:00pm—4:00pm summer

No fee
Appointment required to see material
   not on exhibition

Size of Collection: Approx. 30,000 objects.

Areas of Interest: Focus on the curriculum of the Department of Art and Archaeology, from antiquity to the present. The Mediterranean, western Europe, the United States, Central America, and China are the chief geographical areas.

Women's Material: Less than 1 percent of total. Includes over 200 works of over sixty American women, including sculpture, paintings, drawings, prints, photographs, and pottery. Artists include Mary Cassatt, Anna Hyatt Huntington, Gertrude Kasebier, Alice Neel, Louise Nevelson, and Jane Peterson. The collection also has "Art in Philadelphia", ca. 1788 album of drawings and watercolors, chiefly flower studies, by Mary Harris. The Museum has nineteenth- and twentieth-century works of art as follows:

Drawings
Paintings
Photographs

Pottery
Prints
Sculpture

PSFS   PPSF

Bank Archives
Bank founded 1816

1212 Market Street
Philadelphia, Pa. 19107

(215) 636–6127
Contact: Archivist

By appointment

No fee
Some restrictions

Size of Collection: NA

Areas of Interest: The corporate archives collect and retain materials of historic or long-term importance created and used by the Philadelphia Saving Fund Society, 1816 to the present; the Western Saving Fund Society of Philadelphia, 1847 to 1982; the First Penny Savings Bank John Wanamaker Founder, 1888 to 1931; and the Starr Savings Bank 1879 to 1929.

Women's Material: Depositor records, 1816 to ca. 1900 illustrate women's roles in controlling discretionary income for the household and in acting as trustees for dependent children. The archives also have materials on women in the School Bank program of the mid-twentieth century.

Library, Archive, Museum
Founded 1947

113 West Beechtree Lane	(215) 688–2668
Wayne, Pa. 19087	Contact: President
Tues. 2:00pm—5:00pm; final	No fee
Sun. in month 2:00pm—5:00pm	Materials circulate only to other insti-
By appointment	tutions

Size of Collection: NA

Areas of Interest: The Society's specific interest is in items relating to the history of Radnor Township and the people who lived there, 1682 to the present. Its general interest is in the history of the surrounding area.

Women's Material: References to women are in: The Radnor Township Poor Book (1756–1804); the "Bulletin" of Radnor Historical Society; eighteenth-century tavern licenses, assessment records, and deeds; Mather family account books (1764–1820); the Radnor Library Company minutes (1809–1850); the Dillonstore account books; the minutes of the North Wayne Protective Association (1888–present); the minutes of the South Wayne Public Safety Association; the records of the Harvest Home Fete (1915); and obituaries and school yearbooks (1897–1950). The Society also has a large local photograph file; minute books of the Montgomery Singers; watercolors by Juliet L. Tanner (1833–1909); a doll's house, dolls, and accessories; clothes; six scrapbooks kept by women (1890–1920); two volumes of bound sheet music (1854–1864) owned by Mrs. W. H. Sayen; a large needlework picture by Parmelia A. Roberts exhibited in the Women's Building at the Centennial and recently at the Smithsonian; and scrapbooks containing a series of articles on local history by Emma Patterson (ca. 1947–1953). The Society has printed and handwritten materials in the following areas:

Art, Architecture, Decorative Arts	Minorities and Ethnicity
Behavior	Performing Arts
Charities	Religion
Domestic Activity	Social Life
Education	Statistics
Literature	Work

It also has artifacts as follows:

Appliances and Equipment	Paintings
Clothing and Accessories	Photographs
Drawings	Sculpture
Furniture	Textiles
Household Items	Toys and Amusements

RELIGIOUS SISTERS OF MERCY PMeRSM

Roman Catholic Religious Congregation Archive
Established in Philadelphia 1861

515 Montgomery Avenue	(215) 664–6650
Merion, Pa. 19066	Contact: Secretary General/Archivist
Mon.—Fri. 9:00am—5:00pm	No fee
	Permission required for use

Size of Collection: 4 rooms.

Areas of Interest: History of the religious community, 1861 to the present, includes material on the personal lives of sisters, legal aspects of the community, educational history, financial records, and the foundation of the community in Philadelphia.

Women's Material: 100 percent of total. Includes personal effects of Mary Patricia Waldron, the founder, sisters' dissertations, annals of convents, scrapbooks, and pictures of sisters. The archive has nineteenth- and twentieth-century printed and handwritten materials in the following areas:

Art, Architecture, Decorative Arts   Performing Arts
Literature   Religion

It also has twentieth-century artifacts as follows:

Clothing and Accessories   Photographs
Drawings   Religious Artifacts
Furniture   Sculpture
Paintings

See Hinding 14,874*

ROSEMONT COLLEGE—INSTITUTE OF STUDIES ON THE SOCIETY OF THE HOLY CHILD JESUS PRosC-I

Study Center with archival, library, and audio/visual materials
(See also Holy Child Archives—American Province)
Founded 1969

1341 Montgomery Avenue   (215) 527–0918
Rosemont, Pa. 19010   Contact: Co-Director

By appointment   No fee
                                   No circulation

Published Guides: *The Spirituality of Cornelia Connelly;* "Chronology of the Life of Cornelia Connelly," *SOURCE* 8:1978; Indexes to the Oral History Collection of the Archives of the Society of the Holy Child Jesus and to the Slide Collection on the life and achievements of Cornelia Connelly and the Society of the Holy Child Jesus.

Size of Collection: Approx. 50 vols. and 100 file folders.

Areas of Interest: The life and achievements of Cornelia Connelly (1809–1879), her family (settled in Philadelphia 1732), and the Society of the Holy Child Jesus, which she founded at Derby, England in 1846. The collection includes material on Connelly's institutions for spiritual—chiefly educational—ministries which spread throughout England and to the United States in 1862, to France in 1870, and to Italy, Ireland, Wales, Nigeria, Ghana, Lesotho, Chile, and Mexico in the twentieth century.

Women's Material: 100 percent of total. Includes published and manuscript biographies, theses, and research papers, including eleven published volumes of *SOURCE: Studies and Reflections on the Heritage of the Society of the Holy Child Jesus,* from 1970 to the present. The Institute also has a collection of 1,200 slides on the life and achievements of Cornelia Connelly and the Society of the Holy Child Jesus, with emphasis on her American, especially Philadelphia, heritage; and a printed map of "Cornelia's Philadelphia" 1732 to 1831, showing sites of her own and her family's history as these relate to the sites and movements of the nation's and city's history. The collection includes late nineteenth- and twentieth-century printed, handwritten, and audio/visual material in the following areas:

Art, Architecture, Decorative Arts   Law
Education   Religion
Family Correspondence

The Institute also has numerous photographs and some paintings of Cornelia Connelly and her family.

ROSEMONT COLLEGE—LIBRARY   PRosC

College Library (See also Institute of the Society of the Holy Child Jesus Studies and Holy Child Archives—American Province)
Founded 1922

Rosemont, Pa. 19010   (215) 527–0200
                          Contact: Librarian

Mon.—Fri. 9:00am—5:00pm   No fee
                          Some restrictions

Size of Collection: 139,376 vols.
Areas of Interest: General college collection for use of faculty and students.
Women's Material: Covers the Society of the Holy Child Jesus and its members and Rosemont College and its faculty. The collection also has traditional books by and about women. One drawer of about 2,000 cards is devoted to holdings under "Women" and its various subheadings which are to be found in the regular collection. The Library includes nineteenth- and twentieth-century printed materials in the following areas:

Biography   Religion
Education   Religious Society Studies
History of Women   Sciences
Literature   Social Life
Performing Arts

ROSENBACH MUSEUM AND LIBRARY   PPRF

Library, Archive, Museum
Founded 1954

2010 Delancey Place   (215) 732–1600
Philadelphia, Pa. 19103   Contact: Curator

Tours: Tues.—Sun. 11:00am—4:00pm   Tours: $2.50
Readers: Mon.—Fri. 9:00am—5:00pm   Readers by appointment only
By appointment

Published Guides: *A Selection from Our Shelves.*
Size of Collection: 175,000 items.
Areas of Interest: General collection of British and American literature and Americana, ca. A.D. 900 to 1950.
Women's Material: 15 percent of total. The Marianne Moore Collection contains personal papers, the library, and artifacts owned by the poet (1887–1972) and relating to her family in Missouri, Pennsylvania, and New York (1850–1972). Included are poetry manuscripts, notebooks, correspondence with family members and writers (T. S. Eliot, Ezra Pound, William Carlos Williams, etc.) of the first half of the twen-

tieth century. Miss Moore's living room has been faithfully installed, and the collection contains personal, household, and decorative items. The Library has a large collection of twentieth-century printed and handwritten materials related to literature. The Museum has nineteenth- and twentieth-century artifacts as follows:

Clothing and Accessories	Paintings
Drawings	Photographs
Furniture	Sculpture
Household Items	Toys and Amusements
Musical Instruments	

See Hinding 15,169–15,170

RUTGERS UNIVERSITY—ALEXANDER LIBRARY   NjR-AL

University Library
Founded 1766

Alexander Library	(201) 932–7510/7527
New Brunswick, N.J. 08903	Contact: Coordinator, Dept. of Special
	Collections & Archives
Mon.—Fri. 9:00am—5:00pm;	No fee
Wed. to 9:00pm;	Some individual collections restricted
Sat. 12:00noon—6:00pm	

Published Guides: *Guide to Manuscript Collection; Guide to Manuscript Diaries; Checklist of New Jersey Periodicals; Union List of New Jersey Annual Publications.*
Size of Collection: NA
Areas of Interest: Generally New Jersey social and political materials dating from the seventeenth century to the present.
Women's Material: Approx. 10 percent of total. Includes a good collection of nineteenth century diaries and several periodicals of women's organizations in New Jersey. The Library has nineteenth- and twentieth-century printed and hand-written materials in the following areas:

Behavior	Politics
Charities	Religion
Domestic Activity	Social Life
Education	

See Hinding 10,928–11,064

RUTGERS UNIVERSITY—MABEL SMITH DOUGLASS LIBRARY   NjR-DL

College Library
Founded 1918

Chapel Drive	(201) 932–9407
New Brunswick, N.J. 08903	Contact: Director
Mon.—Fri. 8:00am—4:30pm	No fee
	Limited use of manuscripts in Stanton
	Collection

Size of Collection: 180,000 books.

Areas of Interest: The general collection supports the curriculum of Douglass College (four-year liberal arts with women's studies) and Cook College (school of primarily agricultural and environmental sciences).

Women's Material: Approx. 5 percent of total. The Elizabeth Cady Stanton Papers of the Theodore Stanton Collection contain five original manuscripts ("Fashionable Women/Shipwreck," "Heredity," "Marriage and Divorce," "Homelife," and "Positivists in London"). It also has 581 typed letters of Stanton correspondence, approximately 100 original letters to or mentioning Stanton, and four original Stanton letters. The collection includes assorted broadsides, pamphlets, and photographs.

See Hinding 10,931–10,933

RYAN MEMORIAL LIBRARY ARCHIVES AND HISTORICAL COLLECTIONS
POvR

Library, Archive, Museum
Saint Charles Borromeo Seminary founded 1832, American Catholic Historical Society founded 1884

Saint Charles Borromeo Seminary	(215) 839–3760 ext. 283
Overbrook, Philadelphia, Pa. 19151	Contact: Archivist and Curator
By appointment	No fee

Size of Collection: 400,000 manuscripts, 30,000 books, 2,000 museum items.

Areas of Interest: Catholicism in America from the seventeenth century to the present, emphasizing the Middle Atlantic region, especially Pennsylvania, New Jersey, Delaware, and Maryland. The collection includes books, manuscripts, art, utilitarian objects, newspapers, parish records, and records of societies and seminaries.

Women's Material: 30 percent of total. Includes records and publications of women's religious organizations, manuscripts of Catholic lay women, records of charitable and educational institutions, and decorative and religious art made by women. The Collections have material from the seventeenth century to the present in the following areas:

Charities	Religion
Education	Statistics
Feminism and Reform	

They also have eighteenth- and nineteenth-century artifacts as follows:

Clothing and Accessories	Religious Artifacts
Household Items	Textiles
Paintings	Toys and Amusements
Prints	

ROBERT W. RYERSS LIBRARY AND MUSEUM   PPRL

Library, Museum
Founded 1910

Cottman and Central Avenues	(215) 745–3061
Philadelphia, Pa. 19111	Contact: Librarian and Facility Supervisor

Library: Fri.—Sun. 10:00am—5:00pm

Museum: Sun. 1:00pm—4:00pm

Wed.—Sun. 9:00am—6:00pm

By appointment

No fee, donations welcome

Use for research purposes in building with librarian's permission

Size of Collection: Library 15,000 items, museum 3,000 items.

Areas of Interest: Public lending library; 2,000 volume Victorian family library, nineteenth-century decorative arts collections.

Women's Material: Approx. 15 percent of total. The nineteenth-century personal library of Ann Waln Ryerss includes typical novels and domestic science books. The early twentieth-century public library collection has books in the same areas. The Museum has collections developed by Mary Ryerss Bawn, ca. 1900. Other collections of nineteenth-century family chinaware, glassware, and metalware provide material culture evidence for women's lives. The Library has nineteenth-century handwritten journals and scrapbooks and material on domestic activity as well as printed literature and books on religion. The Museum has eighteenth- and nineteenth-century artifacts as follows:

Appliances and Equipment

Clothing and Accessories

Furniture

Household Items

Paintings

Photographs

Sculpture

Toys and Amusements

SCHOOL DISTRICT OF PHILADELPHIA—PEDAGOGICAL LIBRARY   PPSD

Library

School District founded 1818, Library founded 1883

21st Street South of the Parkway

Philadelphia, Pa. 19103

Mon.—Fri. 8:45am—5:00pm

(215) 299–7783

Contact: Librarian

No fee

Circulates only to employees of Phila. School District

Published Guides: Monthly flyers listing selected titles of new acquisitions.

Size of Collection: 48,000 books.

Areas of Interest: Concentrates in the field of public school education (K–12). The Library also has archival material on Philadelphia schools from 1818.

Women's Material: Less than 1 percent of total. Includes biographical material on women who have been prominent in the history of the Philadelphia school system. The collection also has books, periodicals, and some pictures.

SCHOOL OF NURSING, HOSPITAL OF THE UNIVERSITY OF PENNSYLVANIA
PU-HSN

Nursing School Archive

Nursing School founded 1886, closed 1978

Contact: Chairman, History & Archives, School of Nursing Alumni Assn.

Access at present restricted to graduates of the school

Size of Collection: NA

Areas of Interest: Materials related to nursing, the school, and graduates and friends, 1886 to 1978. The geographical concentration is on Philadelphia.

Women's Material: 95 percent of total. Includes the history of the school, *The First Fifty Years, Training School for Nurses, Hospital of the University of Pennsylvania,* and textbooks written by graduates of the school. The collection also has a small chest that belonged to Florence Nightingale.

THE SHIPLEY SCHOOL—ALUMNI ASSOCIATION   PBmS

Independent Day School (K–12) Archive
Founded 1894

813 Yarrow Street	(215) 525–4544
Bryn Mawr, Pa. 19010	Contact: Alumni Coordinator
Mon.—Fri. 8:30am—4:30pm	No fee

Size of Collection: NA

Areas of Interest: Records of private school for girls (and boys beginning in 1972), 1894 to the present.

Women's Material: The records include correspondence, photographs, catalogues, yearbooks, and biographical files relating to the school from its inception to the present. The archive also has material on the Misses Shipley, Howland, and Brownell, founders and early administrators. The archive has printed, handwritten, and audio/visual material in the following areas, 1894 to the present (Work is current only):

Domestic Activity	Performing Arts
Education	Work

It also has photographs covering the same period.

SISTERS OF THE BLESSED SACRAMENT FOR INDIANS AND COLORED PEOPLES (MOTHERHOUSE)   PBeSBS

Roman Catholic Religious Congregation Library, Archive, Museum
Founded 1891

Saint Elizabeth Convent	(215) 464–9600
1663 Bristol Pike	Contact: Archivist
Bensalem, Pa. 19020	
Library: Mon.—Fri. 10:00am—4:00pm	No fee
Archive: Mon.—Fri. 9:00am—4:00pm	Some archival material restricted

Size of Collection: Library 28,000 vols.; Archive 174 boxes, 59 vols., other miscellaneous material.

Areas of Interest: The library has a general collection to assist sisters. The archive deals with education of American blacks and Indians, 1891 to the present, schools, and social service centers. It also has records, diaries, and journals of Mother Katharine Drexel, Elizabeth Drexel Smith, and Louise Drexel Morrell. Congregational annals include records of closed houses, newspaper articles, jubilee booklets, etc.

Women's Material: 100 percent of total. The most significant material includes correspondence between Superiors General and missionaries and records of work of individual sisters. The collection has nineteenth- and twentieth-century printed and handwritten materials in the following areas:

Education	Performing Arts
Literature	Religion
Minorities and Ethnicity	

It also has a few twentieth-century paintings and religious artifacts.

See Hinding 14,781

SISTERS OF JESUS CRUCIFIED—REGINA MUNDI PRIORY   PDeSJC

Roman Catholic Convent
Established in Philadelphia 1955

Waterloo and Fairfield Roads	(215) 688–5130
Devon, Pa. 19333	Contact: Prioress
By appointment	No fee
	Some restrictions

Size of Collection: Small.

Areas of Interest: Religious community of women who live a monastic life in the tradition of Saint Benedict, concentrating on prayer (in common, including Mass and the singing of the Liturgy of the Hours, as well as individual prayer), silence, solitude, and a strong community spirit. This was the first and one of only a few religious communities to accept as full members women who have certain types of physical limitations (as well as those in good health).

Women's Material: 100 percent. Records of the Priory illustrate the community's approach to life and the offering of a monastic lifestyle to those who had tradition-ally been excluded. The most valuable artifact is a hand-painted and -bound illu-minated book for use in worship. The collection includes twentieth-century (from the 1930s on) printed and handwritten materials in the following areas:

Behavior	Religion
Data on foundation of the Priory	Statistics
Domestic Activity	Work

The Priory also has a number of photographs, slides, and religious artifacts, notably fifty to one hundred hand-bound books.

See Hinding 14,782

SISTERS OF SAINT BASIL THE GREAT, SACRED HEART PROVINCE
PPOSBM

Roman Catholic (Byzantine Rite) Religious Congregation Archive
Established in Philadelphia 1911

710 Fox Chase Road	(215) 342–4221
Philadelphia, Pa. 19111	Contact: Provincial Superior
By appointment	No fee
	Some records restricted

Size of Collection: 115 Record Groups.

Areas of Interest: The holdings are directly related to the history of the Sacred Heart Province of the Sisters of Saint Basil the Great, and/or indirectly to the Order of Saint Basil the Great (dating to the fourth century.)

Women's Material: Approx. 80 percent of total. Includes personal letters and papers of Mother Helen Langevich, the pioneer sisters, major superiors, and later provincials. The archive has records of religious houses of the province, catachetical and Ukrainian language night schools, academies, and care of orphans and retreat work. The collection also includes ecclesiastical art and vestments made by members of the community according to the Ukrainian Byzantine rite.

See Hinding 15,177

SISTERS OF SAINT JOSEPH OF PHILADELPHIA   PPSSJ

Roman Catholic Religious Congregation Archive (See also Chestnut Hill College)
Established in Philadelphia 1847

Germantown and Northwestern Avenues   (215) 248–7200
Philadelphia, Pa. 19118   Contact: Curator of Archives

Mon.—Fri. 8:30am—3:00pm   No fee
By appointment

Size of Collection: 335 cu. ft.

Areas of Interest: Manuscripts and memorabilia relating to the Sisters of Saint Joseph and their work along the eastern seaboard of the United States, 1847 to the present. The archive also has background material and primitive documents dating from the congregation's foundation in France in 1650 to its establishment in the United States in 1836.

Women's Material: 98 percent of total. The records show the growth, development, and achievements of the Philadelphia congregation. They include financial and personnel records, correspondence, photographs, scrapbooks, etc. The archive has twentieth- and some nineteenth-century materials (most printed) in the following areas:

Behavior	Minorities and Ethnicity
Charities	Performing Arts
Education	Psychology
Feminism and Reform	Religion
History	Sciences
Law	Textiles
Literature	Work
Mathematics	

It also has nineteenth- and twentieth-century artifacts as follows:

Clothing and Accessories	Prints
Furniture	Religious Artifacts
Household Items	Samplers
Paintings	Sculpture
Photographs	

See Hinding 15,178*

SISTERS, SERVANTS OF THE IMMACULATE HEART OF MARY, VILLA MARIA HOUSE OF STUDIES PImIHM

Roman Catholic Religious Congregation Archive
Established in Pennsylvania 1858

Kings Road
Immaculata, Pa. 19345

(215) 647–2160
Contact: Archivist

Mon.—Fri. 9:00am—12:00noon;
    1:00pm—3:00pm

No fee
Restricted

Size of Collection: 315 cu. ft.

Areas of Interest: Records of the religious congregation of women dedicated to the apostolate of teaching, established in 1845 in Michigan and 1858 in Pennsylvania, with schools in nine states, Peru, and Chile since 1923.

Women's Material: 100 percent of total. Records on internal activities as a religious congregation, external works in education. The archive has nineteenth- and twentieth-century printed and handwritten materials in the following areas:

Education   Statistics
Literature   Work
Religion

It also has nineteenth- and twentieth-century paintings and religious artifacts and a large number of photographs.

See Hinding 14,859

SISTERS OF THE VISITATION OF HOLY MARY PPVHM

Roman Catholic Cloistered Contemplative Congregation
Established in Philadelphia 1926

5820 City Avenue
Philadelphia, Pa. 19131

(215) 473–5888
Contact: Sister Librarian

By appointment

No fee
No circulation

Size of Collection: Approx. 700 items.

Areas of Interest: Records of the Philadelphia community of the order founded in France in 1610, established in Mexico in 1898, exiled and given refuge in Philadelphia in 1926.

Women's Material: 100 percent of total. Includes annual letters, circular letters, scrapbooks, and clippings. The collection has twentieth-century printed materials on literature and religion. It also has twentieth-century paintings (most religious), photographs, and textiles.

See Hinding 15,147

E. R. SQUIBB & SONS, INC.   NjPS

Pharmaceutical Company Archive, Museum
Company founded 1858

Box 4000   (609) 921–4261
Princeton, N.J. 08540   Contact: Director, U.S. Public Affairs

By appointment   No fee

Size of Collection: NA

Areas of Interest: Artifacts, including advertisements, business documents, and personal papers and possessions of the company founder, relating to the ethical and over-the-counter products of the firm.

Women's Material: Depiction of women as consumers in early advertisements.

SWARTHMORE COLLEGE—FRIENDS HISTORICAL LIBRARY   PSC-Hi

Library, Archive
Founded 1871

Swarthmore College   (215) 447–7496
Swarthmore, Pa. 19081   Contact: Director

Mon.—Fri. 8:30am—4:30pm;   No fee
  Sat. 9:00am—12:00noon during   Open to qualified researchers
  academic year
Closed August

Published Guides: *Catalog of the Books and Serials Collections of the Friends Historical Library; Guide to the Manuscript Collections of Friends Historical Library of Swarthmore College.*

Size of Collection: 34,176 vols., 1,968 doc. boxes of manuscripts.

Areas of Interest: Books, manuscripts, and archives of the Religious Society of Friends (Quakers) from its beginning in England, ca. 1650 and its spread to the American colonies starting in 1656. Included are original records of Friends meetings in Pennsylvania, New Jersey, Delaware, Maryland, Ohio, and Illinois, and microfilm copies of records of many meetings in New York, New England, and North Carolina. The collections reflect the varied activities of Quakers in literature, science, abolition of slavery, Indian rights, the women's movement, peace, education, mental health, prison reform, and temperance.

Women's Material: Approx. 10–20 percent of total. Includes women's minutes of Friends meetings; journals and diaries of over seventy women (mostly concerning spiritual matters); family papers emphasizing genealogy and home life; papers of women leaders active in reform efforts, particularly women's rights, education, abolition of slavery, and peace; and records of charities operated by women largely for the benefit of women or children. The collection also has papers of Lucretia Mott (1793–1880) on antislavery and women's rights; Graceanna Lewis (1821–1912) on science, art, education, and women's rights; and Emily Howland (1827–1929) on women's rights, social reform, and education.

See Hinding 15,268–15,297

SWARTHMORE COLLEGE PEACE COLLECTION PSC-P

Library, Archive
Founded 1930

Swarthmore College
Swarthmore, Pa. 19081

(215) 447–7557
Contact: Curator

Mon.—Fri. 8:30am—4:30pm;
  Sat. 9:00am—12:00noon
Closed August

No fee
Some collections restricted

Published Guides: *Guide to the Archival Collections.*

Size of Collection: 130 major document groups, over 1,500 collections maintained in two collective document groups, over 1,800 periodical series, approx. 8,000 vols.

Areas of Interest: Materials relating to peace. The collection is exclusively devoted to the papers of individuals and the records of organizations committed to the establishment of world peace through disarmament, pacifism, conscientious objection, non-violent social change, or other such peace-related activities and/or mechanisms.

Women's Material: Over 50 percent of book collection, plus significant portion of major document groups. Papers of the following, among others, are included: Jane Addams, Hannah J. Bailey, Emily Greene Balch, Dorothy Detzer, Rose Dabney Forbes, A. Ruth Fry, Hannah Clothier Hull, Belva Lockwood, Lucia Ames Mead, Mildred Scott Olmsted, Tracey Mygatt, Frances Witherspoon, Anna Garlin Spencer, Helene Stoecker, and Lydia G. Wentworth. The collection also has records of such groups that have been led exclusively or significantly by women as the American Union Against Militarism, Another Mother for Peace, Art for World Friendship, Committee on Militarism in Education, People's Mandate to Governments to End War, War Resisters League, Women Strike for Peace, Women's Committee to Oppose Conscription, Women's International League for Peace and Freedom, the Women's Peace Society, Women's Peace Union, and World Peace Foundation, among many others.

See Hinding 15,298–15,317

TEMPLE UNIVERSITY LIBRARIES—SPECIAL COLLECTIONS—CONTEMPORARY CULTURE COLLECTION PPT-CC

Library
Founded 1969

Temple University Library
Philadelphia, Pa. 19122

(215) 787–8667
Contact: Curator

Hours and access vary
Call for appointment

No fee

Size of Collection: 9,000 titles.

Areas of Interest: Alternative, small, and independent press publications and ephemera.

Women's Material: 10 percent of total. Publications from second wave feminist organizations and publishers, including issues of "SPAZM", published by the Sophia Perovskaya and Andrei Zhelyabov Memorial Society of People's Freedom through Women's Liberation, also "Off Our Backs," "Chrysalis," and "Sinister Wisdom."

Library, Archive
Founded 1946

Temple University Library
Philadelphia, Pa. 19122

(215) 787–8240
Contact: Curator, Conwellana-Templana
Collection

Mon.—Fri. 9:00am—5:00pm

No fee
Some collections restricted

Size of Collection: 18,000 vols., 825 lin. ft.

Areas of Interest: As the University Archives of Temple University, the Conwellana-Templana Collection attempts to obtain all possibly useful information and materials pertaining to the University and to all of the personnel associated with it. The collection covers the late nineteenth and twentieth centuries, and concentrates chiefly on southeastern Pennsylvania. It includes publications and personal papers of Temple faculty and alumni.

Women's Material: 35 percent of total. Most significant are the papers of Laura Horner Carnell, Secretary of the University Corporation, who kept the University running effectively from the late 1890s to 1929. The University Hospital archive includes records of the Hospital Training School for Nurses, the Women's Club, and the Greatheart Society, auxiliary to the Hospital Maternity Department. Together, these records illustrate the philanthropic and support role of the women involved, but underline their secondary place in the University and social structure. The Collection has twentieth-century printed, handwritten, and audio/visual materials in the following areas:

Art, Architecture, Decorative Arts
Behavior
Charities
Education
Feminism and Reform
Law
Literature

Medicine
Performing Arts
Religion
Sciences
Social Life
Work

It has nineteenth- and twentieth-century artifacts as follows:

Clothing and Accessories
Diplomas
Furniture
Paintings
Photographs

Scrapbooks
Sculpture
Toys and Amusements
Trophies

See Hinding 15,182–15, 197*

See Hinding 15,182–15, 197*

TEMPLE UNIVERSITY LIBRARIES—SPECIAL COLLECTIONS—PASKOW
SCIENCE FICTION COLLECTION   PPT-P

Library
Founded 1897

Temple University Library
Philadelphia, Pa. 19122

(215) 787–8230
Contact: Head of Special Collections

Mon.—Fri. 9:00am—5:00pm   No fee

Published Guides: Manuscript Register Series, exhibition catalogue.

Size of Collection: 10,000 vols, 100 cu. ft. manuscripts.

Areas of Interest: Primarily twentieth-century science fiction novels. The collection also includes magazines related to the genre, earlier works about imaginary voyages, and some works of fantasy. The professional papers of writers and the archives of publishers of science fiction are actively sought.

Women's Material: The professional papers of Pamela Sargent (1948–   ), science fiction writer.

*See Hinding 15,199**

TEMPLE UNIVERSITY LIBRARIES—SPECIAL COLLECTIONS—RARE BOOKS AND MANUSCRIPTS COLLECTION   PPT-R

Library
Founded 1897

Temple University Library   (215) 787–8230
Philadelphia, Pa. 19122   Contact: Head of Special Collections

Mon.—Fri. 8:30am—4:30pm   No fee

Published Guides: Manuscript Register Series.

Size of Collection: 20,000 vols., 50 lin. ft.

Areas of Interest: Twentieth-century literature, particularly Georgian and Imagist authors, Symbolist literature, Gothic romances; nineteenth- and twentieth-century printing, publishing, and bookselling history. The Collection also includes business history, eighteenth-century religious and parliamentary history, lithography, book illustration, and fine printing.

Women's Material: The Ree Dragonette Papers (New York based metaphysical poet, 1918–   ) include manuscripts of poetry and correspondence with other poets and with editors. The Naomi Royde-Smith (British novelist, 1856–1964) Papers include diaries containing correspondence with other writers and showing her social life in the literary circle in which she moved. The Gertrude Traubel Papers (musician and daughter of Horace Traubel, one of Walt Whitman's literary executors) reflect her own activities, including editing of her father's study of Whitman, *Walt Whitman in Camden,* as well as the activities of her parents.

See Hinding 15,198

TEMPLE UNIVERSITY LIBRARIES—SPECIAL COLLECTIONS—URBAN ARCHIVES CENTER   PPT-U

Archive
Founded 1967

Paley Library   (215) 787–8257
Temple University   Contact: Curator
Philadelphia, Pa. 19122

Mon.—Fri. 9:00am—5:00pm   No fee
                                   Some collections restricted

Published Guides: *Guide to Philadelphia Social Service Collections at the Urban Archives; Housing Association of Delaware Valley: A Guide to the Collection.*
Size of Collection: 4,000 cu. ft.
Areas of Interest: Records relating to the Philadelphia metropolitan area since the mid-nineteenth century. The Collection includes materials on blacks, ethnics, social services, housing, community organizations, business and economic development, labor, crime and the legal system, education, politics, and planning. It has particular strengths in social history, especially immigrants, minorities, social service institutions, and the working classes.
Women's Material: 15 percent of total. The records of the central and various branches of the YWCA (including Germantown, Southwest, and Kensington) offer particularly revealing portraits of the Y's patrician leadership and its relationship to black, immigrant, and working class Philadelphia women. Settlement house collections (including Reed Street Neighborhood House, Houston Community Center, and University settlements) add considerably in filling out this picture. The Mary Foley Grossman Papers and the Amalgamated Clothing Workers records document the activities of women in organized labor, while the Pennsylvania Nurses Association records capture women in a different occupational setting. The Midnight Mission records (for unwed mothers), Sheltering Arms (for women and children), and Women Organized Against Rape show women's activities in other situations. The Collection has nineteenth- and twentieth-century printed, handwritten, and some audio/visual material in the following areas:

Charities	Minorities and Ethnicity
Domestic Activity	Performing Arts
Education	Politics
Feminism and Reform	Settlements
Labor Unions	Sex
Law	Social Life
Medicine	Work

See Hinding 15,200–15,210

UNIVERSITY OF DELAWARE—ARCHIVES   DeU-A

University Archive
Founded 1969

78 East Delaware Avenue	(302) 738–2750
Newark, Del. 19711	Contact: University Archivist
Mon.—Fri. 8:00am—4:30pm	No fee
	Use restricted to scholarly research

Size of Collection: 6,000 cu. ft.
Areas of Interest: Records of the University of Delaware.
Women's Material: Includes records of the Office of the Dean of Women from 1946 to 1969; Masters theses and Doctoral dissertations from 1934 to 1981. Among the theses and dissertations by women are some that cover the following areas:

Behavior	Medicine
Domestic Activity	Minorities and Ethnicity
Education	Sex
Feminism and Reform	Work
Literature and Criticism	

UNIVERSITY OF DELAWARE—WOMEN'S STUDIES PROGRAM   DeU-Wm

Archive
Established 1974

333 Smith Hall
Newark, Del. 19711

Mon.—Fri. 8:30am—4:30pm

(302) 738–8474
Contact: Program Coordinator

No fee
No circulation

Size of Collection: 100 vols., 6 file drawers (clippings).
Areas of Interest: Topics on Women's Studies.
Women's Material: 100 percent of total. Early 1970s women's movement periodicals and pamphlets and educational material (course guides, syllabi, etc.).

UNIVERSITY OF PENNSYLVANIA—ARCHIVES   PU-A

University Archive
University chartered as the College, Academy, and Charitable School in the Province of Pennsylvania 1755, Archive founded 1945

North Arcade Franklin Field E-6
Philadelphia, Pa. 19104

Mon.—Fri. 9:00am—5:00pm
Summer to 4:30pm

(215) 898–7024/25
Contact: University Archivist

No fee

Published Guides: *Guide to the Archives of the University of Pennsylvania from 1740 to 1820.*
Size of Collection: NA
Areas of Interest: Non-current manuscript, printed, and iconographic records, films, tapes, and memorabilia of all divisions of the University of Pennsylvania and of its constituencies (students, alumni, faculty, employees, administrators, and trustees) from 1740 to the present.
Women's Material: Includes biographical files on approximately 10,000 deceased women—former students, faculty members, administrators, honorary degree recipients, and trustees of the University, ca. 1876 to the present (often containing photographs). The archive also has scrapbooks kept by former women students from the late nineteenth and early twentieth centuries; administrative files and correspondence of the former College for Women, School of Education, old Society of Alumnae, Faculty Tea Club, and other campus divisions or organizations predominantly female in orientation or activity. It has substantial "general information" files on "Women at Penn" which include miscellaneous printed and manuscript materials covering women's activities (social, organizational, governmental, athletic) in many spheres of campus life. The Archives have nineteenth- and twentieth-century printed, handwritten, and some audio/visual material in the following areas:

Athletics
Education
Minorities and Ethnicity

Sciences
Social Life

They also have a large collection of photographs.

Museum
Founded 1887

33rd and Spruce Streets	(215) 898–4000
Philadelphia, Pa. 19104	Contact: Director
Tues.—Sat. 10:00am—5:00pm	Contribution
Sun. 1:00pm—5:00pm	Research in collections by appointment

Published Guides: *Guide to the Collections,* also monographs and articles on individual objects or groups of objects.
Size of Collection: Approx. 1 million artifacts.
Areas of Interest: The Museum specializes in archaeology and anthropology and has collections of archaeological and ethnographic nature from the Near East, Egypt, the Mediterranean, the Middle East, Africa, Asia, North, Central, and South America, Europe, and the Pacific. The time period covers the Palaeolithic (200,000 B.C.) to the twentieth century A.D.
Women's Material: From all the above-listed geographical areas the Museum has objects used by women (especially household items and costumes), depicting women (paintings, sculpture), or describing women's activities (Egyptian papyri, cuneiform tablets). Many of the materials were collected by women archaeologists or anthropologists, or were donated to the Museum by women.

UNIVERSITY OF PENNSYLVANIA—THE UNIVERSITY MUSEUM—ARCHIVES
PU-MA

Museum Archive
Museum founded 1887

33rd and Spruce Streets	(215) 898–8304
Philadelphia, Pa. 19104	Contact: Archivist
Mon.—Fri. 9:00am—4:30pm	No fee

Size of Collection: 2,000 lin. ft.
Areas of Interest: Records of the Museum of archaeology and anthropology. The materials reflect the administrative history of the Museum as well as field work in the United States and abroad from the nineteenth century to the present.
Women's Material: 400 lin. ft. Consists of women's research in archaeology and activity in administration. The collection includes work of Edith Hall Dohan and Harriet Boyd Hawes in Crete, Frederica de Laguna in Alaska, and Elizabeth Ralph, who helped develop Carbon Fourteen dating. It also has records of Sara Yorke Stevenson, a founder of the Museum and first woman curator of Egyptology. The Museum has twentieth-century printed and handwritten material in the following areas:

Art, Architecture, Decorative Arts	Sciences
Education	Work

It also has a collection of watercolors dating from the 1930s.

UNIVERSITY OF PENNSYLVANIA—VAN PELT LIBRARY   PU-V

Library
University chartered as the College, Academy, and Charitable School in the Province of Pennsylvania 1755

3420 Walnut Street
Philadelphia, Pa. 19104

(215) 898–7555
Contact: Librarian

Hours vary throughout year

No fee
Users must have Penn identification card on weekends and weekdays after 6:00pm.

Size of Collection: 3,000,000 vols.
Areas of Interest: Materials to support the present and anticipated needs of the Penn faculty and student body in a wide variety of disciplines, languages, and forms. At present the collection includes more than three million books in many subjects including the humanities, the social sciences, the natural sciences, law, medicine, and dentistry.
Women's Material: The most significant is the microfilm set, "Herstory."

UNIVERSITY OF PENNSYLVANIA—VAN PELT LIBRARY—SPECIAL COLLECTIONS   PU-VS

Library
Founded 1751

3420 Walnut Street
Philadelphia, Pa. 19104

(215) 898–7088/7552
Contact: Assistant Director for Special Collections

Mon.—Fri. 9:00am—5:00pm

No fee
Restricted to legitimate researchers

Published Guides: Brochure on Furness Shakespeare Library.
Size of Collection: 161,000 vols.
Areas of Interest: English Renaissance drama; American drama from the eighteenth century to the present; Spanish drama of the Golden Age; English fiction of the eighteenth and nineteenth centuries; Italian mediaeval and Renaissance literature and history, witchcraft; history of chemistry; history of the Inquisition; early Americana and Canadiana including travel literature.
Women's Material: Approx. 33 percent of total. Collections of English and American fiction from the seventeenth through the nineteenth centuries have works by some 450 recognizable women, plus others who are anonymous or use pseudonyms. Eighty-seven women are represented in the Furness correspondence, including Charlotte Endymion Porter and Agnes Irwin. The Library also has letters, manuscripts, diaries, poetry, and scholarly studies including papers of Philadelphians Marian Anderson, Ada Rehan, and Agnes Repplier. The Drama collection includes works by forty-five American and two European women, as well as works by and about seventeenth-century English women. The theatre collection has letters, playbills, promptbooks, scrapbooks, and photographs covering nineteenth- and twentieth-century actresses. The Edgar Fahs Smith Collection of the History of Chemistry has works by women pioneers in chemistry, including dissertations and Jane Marcet's

1804 *Conversations in Chemistry.* The Henry Charles Lea Library of Mediaeval History includes a collection on witchcraft. The Short Title Catalogue Collection of English books published to 1640 contains an abundance of works for and about women.

VALLEY FORGE NATIONAL HISTORICAL PARK   PVfNHi

Historic Site
Founded 1976

Valley Forge, Pa. 19481   (215) 783–7700

Contact: Chief, Interpretation and Visitor Services

Mon.—Fri. 8:30am—5:00pm   No fee
Appointment necessary to use collections

Published Guides: *Swords and Blades of the American Revolution; Collector's Illustrated Guide of the American Revolution; History of the Weapons of the American Revolution.* None current.
Size of Collection: 1,700 items.
Areas of Interest: The Park commemorates the endurance of General George Washington's Army during the encampment of December 19, 1777 to June 19, 1778. Collections relate to arms, accoutrements, and personal objects of soldiers, civilians of the Valley Forge community (ca. 1710–1780), and the valley forge. A few objects connected with the development of the site as a historic area are preserved.
Women's Material: Less than 1 percent of total. Includes a selection of materials relating to the Centennial and Memorial Association and its efforts to preserve Washington's Headquarters, 1878–1910. Limited library resources have secondary sources on women in the American Revolution, including early printings of eighteenth-century diaries. The collection also includes household utensils, eighteenth-century embroidered purses, an embroidered vest, and some photographs, ca. 1900.

THE VOLUNTEERS FOR THE PHILADELPHIA ORCHESTRA   PPVO

Fund-Raising Organization, Archive, Museum (See also Philadelphia Orchestra
   Association)
Founded 1904

1420 Locust Street #320   (215) 893–1956
Philadelphia, Pa. 19102   Contact: President

By appointment   Loans restricted

Size of Collection: NA
Areas of Interest: Records of The Women's Committees (now Volunteers for the Philadelphia Orchestra) since their inception in 1904. The organization has memorabilia from the Museum of the Academy of Music, pamphlets, programs, papers, etc. pertaining to the musical world.
Women's Material: 100 percent of total. Records of the Women's Committees include minutes, brochures, publications, slide show, etc.

THE WAR LIBRARY AND MUSEUM OF THE MILITARY ORDER OF THE UNITED STATES   PPWL

Library, Archive, Museum
Founded 1886

1805 Pine Street
Philadelphia, Pa. 19103

Mon.—Fri. 10:00am—4:00pm

(215) 735–8196
Contact: Director

Fee: $1.00, senior citizens free
Does not circulate

Size of Collection: 16,000 items.

Areas of Interest: Specializes in every aspect of the Civil War, including the post-Reconstruction period.

Women's Material: 150 items. Includes information on women nurses of the Civil War, spies, rebels, women who fought, all in secondary sources. The War Library also has records of the Dames of the Loyal Legion.

WEST CHESTER UNIVERSITY—FRANCIS HARVEY GREEN LIBRARY   PWcT

Library, Archive
Founded as West Chester Normal School 1871

West Chester University
West Chester, Pa. 19380

Hours vary

(215) 436–3456
Contact: Special Collections Librarian
and Archivist

No fee
Does not circulate

Size of Collection: 6,000 books, plus archive.

Areas of Interest: Materials related to American botany, 1700 to 1900s; Chester County history; writings of faculty and alumni; Chester County authors.

Women's Material: 5 percent of total books, 40 percent of total archives. Since the University began as a Normal School and became a Teachers College, many faculty members and students were women. Most of the archives relate to women and their education. The material includes a picture collection, 1880s to 1940s, on women's athletics and classes; research papers and theses by women students; records of women's athletic and student associations; books by women faculty and alumni; scrapbooks and autograph books of women students, especially 1880s to 1900s; and family photograph albums and diaries of Emma Taylor and Marie Hansen, sister and wife of Bayard Taylor. The Library has nineteenth- and twentieth-century printed, handwritten, and audio/visual materials in the following areas:

Art, Architecture, Decorative Arts	Minorities and Ethnicity
Autograph Albums	Oral Histories
Autographed Books	Performing Arts
Charities	Religion
Domestic Activity	Sciences
Education	Scrap Books
Feminism and Reform	University Archives
Literature	

It also has artifacts as follows:

Clothing and Accessories	Photographs
Drawings	Sculpture
Paintings	

WESTTOWN SCHOOL   PWeW

Independent School, Boarding 9–12, Day K–10
Founded 1799

Westtown School	(215) 399–0123
Westtown, Pa. 19395	Contact: Archivist
By appointment only	Donation appreciated
	No circulation

Size of Collection: 62 manuscript boxes.

Areas of Interest: Letters and memorabilia pertaining to Westtown School, its origin, administration policies, and student life, letters to and from students' families and teachers, and letters of life at Westtown and at home. The collection includes information and advice to parents as recommended by the Philadelphia Yearly Meeting of Friends, which has oversight of the school. The material dates from 1794 to the present, mostly covering the Philadelphia and Chester County area, but also other parts of the Eastern United States.

Women's Material: Approx. 50 percent of total. A collection of approximately ninety samplers made by Quaker girls, 1800 to the 1850s, includes alphabet, darning, and extract samplers. There are also letters written by parents to their children at the school and by children and teachers to their friends at home. The School has eighteenth-, nineteenth-, and twentieth-century materials in the following areas:

Behavior	Religion
Domestic Activity	Sciences
Education	Social Life
Letter Collections	Statistics

It also has eighteenth-, nineteenth-, and twentieth-century artifacts as follows:

Clothing and Accessories	Photographs
Drawings	Textiles
Furniture	

See Hinding 15,347–15,352

WILLET STAINED GLASS STUDIO, INC.   PPWS

Stained Glass Studio Library
Studio founded 1890

10 East Moreland Avenue	(215) 247–5721
Philadelphia, Pa. 19118	Contact: Librarian
Mon.—Fri. 9:00am—4:00pm	No fee
	By appointment, no circulation

Size of Collection: NA

Areas of Interest: Art work and business archives of the Studio. The library also has books, slides, photographs, etc. of general stained glass interest.

Women's Material: Many designs on file were done by women. The librarian is compiling an archive of women working in stained glass, i.e., artist-designers, craftspeople, employees of stained glass studios in administrative positions, and scholars who specialize in stained glass. About 300 entries cover the eighteenth century to the present (although most entries are contemporary), in the United States, Europe, England, Scandinavia, and Japan.

THE HENRY FRANCIS DU PONT WINTERTHUR MUSEUM, INC.—WINTERTHUR ARCHIVES   DeWint-A

Archive, Museum
Founded as Winterthur Museum Archives 1951 and Estate Archives 1969

Winterthur, Del. 19735   (302) 656–8591
                                          Contact: Archivist

Mon.—Fri. 8:30am—4:30pm   No fee
                                          Some restrictions

Size of Collection: Approx. 1,500 lin. ft.
Areas of Interest: Materials related to Henry Francis du Pont, Ruth Wales (Mrs. Henry F. du Pont), Winterthur Farms, Inc., Winterthur Museum, Winterthur Gardens, and the Chestertown House Corporation. The collection also has materials related to Henry du Pont, Louisa Gerhard (Mrs. Henry du Pont), Henry Algernon du Pont, Mary Pauline Foster (Mrs. Henry A. du Pont), Louise Evelina du Pont (Mrs. Francis B. Crowninshield), Alfred Craven Harrison, and the Col. Henry A. du Pont Company. Inclusive dates are 1850s to 1970s, bulk dates are 1900 to 1970.
Women's Material: Approx. 5 percent of total. Includes personal and business correspondence; financial records, including banking and household records; family photographs, travel diaries; social forms, such as invitations, guest lists, place cards, etc.; and sheet music. The majority of the records are from the twentieth century, 1900 to 1967. The Archives have twentieth-century printed and handwritten material in the following areas:

Behavior   Education
Domestic Activity   Social Life

They also have twentieth-century clothing and accessories and photographs.

THE HENRY FRANCIS DU PONT WINTERTHUR MUSEUM, INC.—JOSEPH DOWNS MANUSCRIPT AND MICROFILM COLLECTION   DeWint-D

Museum
Founded 1930

Winterthur, Del. 19735   (302) 656–8591 Ext. 228
                                          Contact: Librarian

Mon.—Fri. 8:30am—4:30pm   No fee
                                          No circulation

Size of Collection: Over 57,000 items.
Areas of Interest: The arts of the United States and Great Britain, 1630 to 1914. The Collection has manuscripts pertaining to the decorative arts, with emphasis on

American craftspeople from the seventeenth through the nineteenth centuries, including household inventories, wills, court records, estate records, bills, account books, diaries, designs and drawings for objects and buildings, import-export records, personal and business letters, letter books, surveys and records of fire insurance companies, etc. Special collections have Shaker materials, greeting and advertising cards, paper toys, and research papers of collectors and writers.

Women's Material: Less than 1 percent of total. Includes family papers (both craftsmen and genealogical, such as the Richardson and allied families of Philadelphia), inventories and wills, accounts, apprenticeship records, deeds, letters (business and social), diaries, commonplace books, memoirs, drawings, silhouettes, recipe books, scrapbooks, and printed materials (advertisements, trade labels, broadsides, and prints). The Collection has seventeenth-, eighteenth-, and nineteenth-century printed and handwritten material in the following areas:

Art, Architecture, Decorative Arts	Law
Domestic Activity	Social Life
Education	Work

THE HENRY FRANCIS DU PONT WINTERTHUR MUSEUM, INC.— LIBRARY—PRINTED BOOK & PERIODICAL COLLECTION   DeWint-L

Museum Library
Founded 1952

Winterthur, Del. 19735   (302) 656–8591 Ext. 301
                                          Contact: Librarian

Mon.—Fri. 8:30am—4:30pm   No fee
                                          No circulation
                                          Interlibrary loan available for non-rare
                                               materials

Published Guides: Printed catalogue.
Size of Collection: 52,000 bound vols.
Areas of Interest: American fine and decorative arts to 1914 and their English and European backgrounds. Also American and other social history.
Women's Material: Includes material by and about American women, both as creators and users of arts, and in the greater context of social history. There are significant holdings of books on the arts by women, books about women in the arts, and about women in their domestic setting. The Collection has printed materials from the seventeenth-century to 1914 in the following areas:

Art, Architecture, Decorative Arts	Literature
Behavior	Social Life
Charities	Technology
Domestic Activity	Work
Education	

WOMEN FOR GREATER PHILADELPHIA   PPWG

Service Organization, Operates Laurel Hill Mansion
Founded as Women for the Bicentennial 1972

530 Walnut Street   (215) 627–1770
Philadelphia, Pa. 19106   Contact: President

Mon.—Fri. 9:00am—5:00pm   Fee: $1.00 by car; $.80 by trolley
Laurel Hill: Wed.—Sun. 10:00am—
    4:00pm

Size of Collection: NA
Areas of Interest: Organization members serve as hostesses at city events, staff
and operate Laurel Hill Mansion, and conduct Museum Showcase.
Women's Material: 100 percent of total. Records, correspondence, releases, and
press clippings related to the organizations. Laurel Hill Mansion illustrates domestic
life of the eighteenth and early nineteenth centuries.

WOMEN'S INSURANCE SOCIETY OF PHILADELPHIA   PPWISP

Trade Organization—Member of the National Association of Insurance Women
Philadelphia Chapter established 1946

Insurance Society   (215) 854–7493
Public Ledger Bldg.   Contact: President
Philadelphia, Pa. 19107

By appointment   No fee

Size of Collection: NA
Areas of Interest: Promotion of insurance education, safety, professionalism in
the insurance industry, and fellowship with other industry members.
Women's Material: 100 percent of total. Records of the organization.

WYCK   PPWy

Museum
House built 1690, established as Museum 1973

6026 Germantown Avenue   (215) 848–1690
Philadelphia, Pa. 19144   Contact: Administrator

Mon.—Fri. 9:00am—5:00pm   No fee
By appointment

Published Guides: Guide to the Collection.
Size of Collection: Over 100,000 manuscripts.
Areas of Interest: Collection of manuscripts, photographs, pamphlets, and related
materials that belonged to the Haines family of Wyck in Germantown. The collection spans seven generations of the family from the mid-eighteenth century through
the mid-twentieth century.
Women's Material: Approx. 40 percent of total. Women's diaries from about 1800
through the early twentieth century include a complete run of diaries written by

Margaret Vaux Wistar Haines from 1874 to 1916. The collection also has eighteenth- and nineteenth-century "receipt" books and much correspondence to and from women. No "famous" women lived at Wyck; the papers are best used as evidence of everyday life for well-educated and wealthy Quaker ladies who had some interest in education, abolition, religious revivalism, and other nineteenth-century social causes. Wyck has printed and handwritten materials from the 1790s to 1915 in the following areas:

Art, Architecture, Decorative Arts	Education
Behavior	Medicine
Charities	Religion
Domestic Activity	Social Life

It has eighteenth-, nineteenth-, and twentieth-century artifacts as follows:

Appliances and Equipment	Household Items
Clothing and Accessories	Photographs
Drawings	Textiles
Furniture	Toys and Amusements

Left to right, top row: Lucretia Mott (Library Company of Philadelphia); Mary Ann Shadd Cary (Moorland-Spingarn Research Center, Howard University); Anna Howard Shaw (Historical Society of Pennsylvania); Rebecca Gratz (Rosenbach Museum and Library); 2nd row: Ann Preston (Archives and Special Collections on Women in Medicine, Medical College of Pennsylvania); Caroline A. Moore (Bachrach); Crystal Byrd Fauset (Acme Newspictures); Sarah Josepha Hale (Historical Society of Pennsylvania); 3rd row: Frances Watkins Harper (Charles Blockson); Sarah Worthington King Peter (Peter Family); M. Carey Thomas (Bryn Mawr College Archives Photograph Collection); Henrietta Bowers Duterte (Felicia Blue); bottom row: Cornelia Connelly (Rosemont College); Eliza Sproat Turner (New Century Guild)

Notable Delaware Valley Women

Until the history of women in the Delaware Valley has been covered in more detail and more work has been done on women of the nineteenth- and twentieth-century immigrant groups, no list of notable women can be complete. The major existing sources for the most part have a bias toward white, Protestant, middle and upper class "mainstream" women and this list, regrettably, shares that fault. Among known women some have been omitted simply because critical information on them could not be found within the constraints of the project. Others could not be included because they did not fulfill one of the criteria.

The criteria for inclusion are as follows: a) must have been born or done significant work in the Delaware Valley area (Philadelphia and contiguous Pennsylvania counties, New Jersey north to New Brunswick, Delaware south to Dover); b) must have died before December 31, 1975 (following the standard set in the fourth volume of *Notable American Women*); c) must be documented in some available primary or secondary source.

Since information can be found elsewhere on all these women, this section is designed to be an index rather than a full biographical dictionary. Each entry indicates where material is available on the subject in local repositories (the code is deciphered in the Index to Institutions), whether there are biographical works listed in the Bibliography (Bib.), and the original source (by a superscript—see below). Women who we know were born in the area are noted with an asterisk (*), members of the American Philosophical Society by a plus sign (+), and Gimbel Award recipients by a number sign (#). Entries taken from *Notable American Women* have no superscript numbers. In most cases they are quoted directly from that work with the permission of Radcliffe College. Those in Volume 4 are noted (v. 4).

SOURCES FOR NOTABLE DELAWARE VALLEY WOMEN

No superscript—*Notable American Women: 1607–1950* ed. Edward T. James, 3 vols., (Cambridge, 1971) and *Notable American Women: The Modern Period*, ed. Barbara Sicherman and Carol Hurd Green (Cambridge, 1980). The latter is noted (v. 4).   1. *Notable Women of Pennsylvania*, ed. Gertrude B. Biddle and Sarah D. Lowrie (Philadelphia, 1942).   2. *The American Woman in Colonial and Revolutionary Times*, by Eugenie Andruss Leonard, Sophie Hutchinson Drinker, and Miriam Young Holden. (Philadelphia, 1962).   3. *Notes on Woman Printers in Colonial America and the U.S.A., 1639–1975*, comp. Marjorie Dana Barlow (Charlottesville, Va., 1976).   4. Miscellaneous journal and magazine articles, suggestions of scholars and institutions, etc.   5. The Afro-American Historical and Cultural Museum   6. Obituary

A

ABBOTT, Elenore Plaisted (1875–1935). Illustrator. PChB, PPPCl.[4]

ADGER, Lucy (b. 1846). Black singer, founder of Sedgwick Opera Co.[5]

AHRENS, Ellen Wetherald (1859–1933). Portrait and miniature artist. PPPCl.[4]

AITKEN, Jane (1764–1832). Printer, bookseller, bookbinder. PHi, PPAmP, PPL.

*ALCOTT, Louisa May (1832–1888). Author. Bib.

ALICE of Dunk's Ferry (1685–1802). Black Quaker oral traditionalist.[5]

ALLEN, Sarah Bass (1764–1849). Black civic leader, worker on Underground Railroad, wife of Richard Allen, founder of Mother Bethel Church.[5]

AMES, Fanny Baker (1840–1931). Charity organizer.

ANDERSON, Caroline Still Wiley (1848–1919). Black educator, physician, writer.[5]

ARCHAMBAULT, Anna Margaretta (1856?–1956). Artist, author, educator. PHi, PPPCl.[4]

ARMBRUESTER, Mrs. Anthony (fl. 1750s). Printer.[3]

ARMSTRONG, Eva (1877–1962). Historian of chemistry, curator. PU-VS.[4]

*ATWELL, Cordelia Jennings (1845–1920). Black educator, first black teacher in Philadelphia public schools.[5]

AUNT FANNY. See GAGE, Frances Dana Barker.

AVERY, Rachel G. Foster (1858–1919). Suffragist.

B

BACHE, Margaret Hartman Markoe. See DUANE, Margaret Hartman Markoe Bache.

*BACHE, Sarah Franklin (1743–1808). Relief worker during Revolutionary War, daughter of Benjamin Franklin. PPAmP.

BACHMAN, Anna Maria Boll. See BACHMAN, Mother Mary Francis.

BACHMAN, Mother Mary Francis (1824–1863). Roman Catholic nun, founder of Congregation of Sisters of St. Francis of Philadelphia. PAsN.[4]

BAILEY, Lydia R. (1779–1869). Printer.[3]

BAKER, Katherine (1876–1919). Writer, World War I nurse.[1]

*BANACH, Sister M. Martina (1907–1971). Roman Catholic nun, artist, educator. PPCSFN.[4]

BARBER, Alice. See STEPHENS, Alice Barber.

*BARRYMORE, Ethel (1879–1959). Actress. PPT-R. Bib. (v. 4).

*BARRYMORE, Georgiana Emma Drew (1854–1893). Actress; mother of Lionel, Ethel, John.

BASCOM, Florence (1862–1945). Geologist. PBm-Geol. Dept.

BAUDUY, Victorine du Pont (b. 1792). Educator, superintendent of Brandywine Manufacturers Sunday School. Bib.[4]

BAWN, Mary Ryerss (1848–1916). Collector, museum founder, philanthropist. PPRL.[4]

*BEAUX, Cecilia (1855–1942). Portrait painter, teacher. PHC, PPD-M, PPMA, PPPAFA. PPPCl. Bib.

BEEKMAN, Lillian Grace (1859–1946). Swedenborgian publicist and philosopher. PBa.[4]

BELLANCA, Dorothy Jacobs (1894–1946). Trade union organizer.

BENBRIDGE, Laetitia Sage (d. ca. 1780). Miniaturist.[2]

*BENDER, Rose I. Magil (1895–1964). Zionist organizer. PPBI.[4]

BENNETT, Alice (1851–1925). Physician, hospital superintendent.

BERGEN, Flora Baston (1870–1906). Black ballad singer, organizer of concert company.[5]

BETTLE, Jane Temple (ca. 1774–1840). Diarist, wife of Quaker minister. PHC.[4]

BEZIAT, Marian. See BEZIAT, Sister Mary Frederick.

BEZIAT, Sister Mary Frederick (1863–1903). Roman Catholic nun, initiated ecumenical Bible classes in Philadelphia. PElDS.[4]

BIDDLE, Rebecca Cornell (1755–ca. 1834). Revolutionary War relief worker.[1]

*BINGHAM, Anne Willing (1764–1801). Federalist society leader. Bib.

BISSELL, Emily Perkins (1861–1948). Social welfare worker, antisuffragist, initiator of antituberculosis Christmas Seal in America. DeHi.

BLACKWELL, Elizabeth (1821–1910). Physician, first woman in modern times to graduate in medicine. Bib.

*BLAKER, Eliza Ann Cooper (1854–1926). Kindergarten educator.

BLANKENBURG, Lucretia Longshore (1845–1937). Suffragist, club-woman, civic reformer.[*] PHi, PP. Bib.

BLOOMFIELD-MOORE, Clara Sophia Jessup. See MOORE, Clara Sophia Jessup.

BLOOR, Ella Reeve (1862–1951). Radical, labor organizer, journalist, suffragist. Bib. (v. 4).

*BLUNT, Katharine (1876–1954). College administrator, home economics educator, nutritionist. (v. 4).

BODLEY, Rachel Littler (1831–1888). Chemist, botanist, Dean of Women's Medical College of Pennsylvania. PPMCP.

*BOGLE, Sarah Comly Norris (1870–1932). Librarian.

BOK, Mary Louise Curtis. See ZIMBALIST, Mary Louise Curtis Bok.

BONNEY, Mary Lucinda (1816–1900). Educator, Indian rights advocate.

*BONSALL, Elizabeth F. (1861–1956). Painter, illustrator. PChB, PPPAFA, PPPCl.[4]

BONSALL, Mary M. (d. 1959). Miniaturist. PPPCl.[4]

BONSTELLE, Jessie (1871–1932). Actress, director, theatre manager.

*BOWEN, Catherine Shober Drinker (1897–1973). Biographer, essayist.[+] PP. (v. 4).

BOYKO, Anna Kobryn (1889–1973). Roman Catholic church worker, founder of Daughters of the Ukraine. PPBI.[4]

BRADFORD, Cornelia Smith (d. 1755). Printer, journalist.

BRANSON, Julia (1889–1970). Quaker teacher, social and foreign relief worker, active in American Friends Service Committee. PSC-Hi.[4]

*BREWSTER, Anne Hampton (1819–1892). Critic and foreign correspondent. PPL. Bib.[4]

BRIDGES, Fidelia (1834–1923). Painter.

BRINGHURST, Hannah (1751–1782). Quaker minister, abolitionist, diarist. PHi.[4]

BRINTON, Anna Shipley (1887–1969). Quaker educator, foreign relief worker, active in American Friends Service Committee. PSC-Hi.[4]

*BROOMALL, Anna Elizabeth (1847–1931). Obstetrician, medical educator. PCDHi, PPMCP.

*BROWN, Charlotte Amanda Blake (1846–1904). Physician and surgeon, founder of San Francisco Children's Hospital.

BROWN, Charlotte Harding (1873–1951). Illustrator. PChB. Bib.[4]

BROWNELL, Eleanor (1876–1968). Educator. PBmS.[4]

BRUNTON, Ann. See MERRY, Ann Brunton.

BUCK, Pearl (1892–1973). Writer.[*] Bib. (v. 4).

BURNHAM, Mary Arthur (1853–1928). Civic leader, club-woman, suffragist.[1]

BUSH-BROWN, Louise Carter (1897–1973). Horticulturist, director of Pennsylvania School of Horticulture for Women.[*] PPT-CT.[4]

BUTLER, Frances Anne Kemble. See KEMBLE, Frances Anne.

*BUTLER, Margaret F. (1861–1931). Physician, teacher.[1]

C

CADBURY, Emma (1875–1965). Quaker social and foreign relief worker, active in American Friends Service Committee. PHC.[4]

*CAMPBELL, Jane (1845–1928). Author, suffragist, club-woman.[1]

*CANNON, Annie Jump (1863–1941). Astronomer. DeHi.[4]

CARNELL, Laura Horner (1867–1929). Educator. PPT-CT.[1]

CARNELL, Mary (d. 1925). Photographer. PPPCl.[4]

*CARSON, Anna Lea Baker (1864–1933). Civic leader.[1]

*CARY, Mary Ann Shadd (1823–1893). Black teacher, journalist, lawyer. Bib.

CASSATT, Mary (1844–1926). Painter. NjP-M, PPMo, PPPAFA, PPPM. Bib.

*CHANDLER, Elizabeth Margaret (1807–1834). Author, abolitionist. Bib.

CHAPIN, Helen (1882–1950). Orientalist. PBm-A.[4]

CIST, Mrs. Carl (fl. 1805). Printer.[3]

CLAGHORN, Louise E. (1832–1898). Civil War relief worker.[1]

CLARKE, Sara Jane. See LIPPINCOTT, Sara Jane Clarke.

CLAYPOOLE, Elizabeth. See ROSS, Betsy.

CLEVELAND, Emeline Horton (1829–1878). Surgeon, medical educator. PHi, PPMCP.

*COATES, Florence Van Leer Earle Nicholson (1850–1927). Poet.

COCHRAN, Ann (fl. 1811). Printer.[3]

*COHEN, Katherine Myrtilla (1859–1914). Sculptor, painter. PPPCl.[1]

*COHEN, Mary Matilda (1854–1911). Civic leader, philanthropist.[1]

COHEN, Matilda Samuel (1820–1888). Civic leader.[1]

*COLE, Rebecca J. (1846–1922). Black physician, teacher, first black graduate of Women's Medical College.[5]

COLES, Bertha Horstmann Lippincott (1880–1963). Author, World War I and II relief worker.* PHi.[4]

*CONNELLY, Cornelia Augusta (1809–1879). Roman Catholic nun, founder of Society of the Holy Child Jesus. PPAmC, PRosC, PRosHC. Bib.

COPPIN, Fanny Marion Jackson (1837–1913). Black educator, foreign missionary. Bib.

CORBIN, Margaret Cochran (1751–1800). Revolutionary War heroine. Bib.

COUSIN ALICE. See HAVEN, Emily Bradley Neal.

*COX, Hannah (1795–1876). Abolitionist.[1]

CRAWFORD, Jane Crawford (1820–1889). Educator.[1]

CRAYDOCK, Ruth. See LLOYD, Elizabeth.

*CRESSON, Sarah (1771–1829). Quaker minister, diarist. PHC.[4]

CURTIS, Louisa Knapp (1855–1920). Editor.[1]

CURTIS, Mary Louise. See ZIMBALIST, Mary Louise Curtis Bok.

CUSHMAN, Charlotte Saunders (1816–1876). Actress, manager of Walnut Street Theatre. PHi. Bib.

D

DARRAGH, Lydia Barrington (1729–1789). Colonial nurse and midwife, Revolutionary War heroine. Bib.

DAVIS, Katharine Bement (1860–1935). Penologist, social worker.

DAVIS, Rebecca Blaine Harding (1831–1910). Author. Bib.

DAY, Anna Blakiston (1869–1952). Reformer, club-woman. PHi.[4]

DAY, Bertha Corson (1875–1968). Illustrator. PChB, PPPCl.[4]

DE CLEYRE, Voltarine (1866–1912). Anarchist, feminist, social reformer, educator. Bib.[4]

DE FORD, Miriam Allen. See SHIPLEY, Miriam Allen De Ford.

DELANO, Jane Arminda (1862–1919). Professional nurse. Hosp. Univ. Pa. Bib.

*DICKINSON, Anna Elizabeth (1842–1932). Civil War orator, lyceum lecturer. PHi. Bib.

DICKSON, Susan Evelyn (1832–1915). Author, journalist, suffragist.[1]

DILLAYE, Blanche (1851–1932). Artist. PPPCl.[1]

DOHAN, Edith Hayward Hall (1877–1943). Classical archaeologist. PU-M.

*DOLLEY, Sarah Read Adamson (1829–1909). Physician, leader of professional women.

DONNELLY, Lucy Martin (1870–1948). Teacher of English, Bryn Mawr College. PBm-A.

DOOLITTLE, Hilda (H.D.) (1886–1961). Poet, writer. PPRF. (v. 4).

DOUGLASS, Mabel Smith (1877–1933). Educator, founder of New Jersey College for Women (Douglass College). NjR-DL.[4]

*DOUGLASS, Sarah Mapps Douglass (1806–1882). Black teacher, journalist, abolitionist. PHi, PSC-Hi.

DREW, Georgiana Emma. See BARRYMORE, Georgiana Emma Drew.

DREW, Mrs. John. See DREW, Louisa Lane.

DREW, Louisa Lane (1820–1897). Actress, theatre manager, mother of Georgiana Emma Drew Barrymore.

*DREXEL, Mother Mary Katharine (1858–1955). Founder, Sisters of the Blessed Sacrament for Indians and Colored People. PBeSBS. Bib. (v. 4).

*DRINKER, Catherine A. (d. 1923). Painter. PPPAFA.[4]

*DRINKER, Elizabeth Sandwith (ca. 1743–1807). Diarist. PHC, PHi. Bib.[1]

DUANE, Margaret Hartman Markoe Bache (fl. 1790s). Publisher of "Aurora".[3]

DUDLEY, Helena Stuart (1858–1932). Settlement worker, pacifist.

DUNCAN, Margaret (1721–1802). Merchant, philanthropist.[1]

DU PONT, Louisa Gerhard (1816–1900). Civic leader, philanthropist. DeWint-A.[4]

*DU PONT, Louise Evelina (1877–1948). Civic leader, philanthropist. DeWint-A.[4]

DU PONT, Mary Pauline Foster (1849–1902). Civic leader, philanthropist. DeWint-A.[4]

DU PONT, Ruth Wales (1889–1967). Civic leader, philanthropist. DeWint-A.[4]

DU PONT, Victorine. See BAUDUY, Victorine du Pont.

*DUTERTE, Henrietta Bowers (1820–1903). Black undertaker, philanthropist.[5]

E

EAKINS, Susan MacDowell (1851–1938). Painter. PPPAFA. Bib.[4]

ELLET, Mary Israel (ca. 1776–1885). Patriot.[1]

*ELLSLER, Effie (1854?–1942). Actress.

ELY, Gertrude S. (1876–1970). Leader in social, political, and welfare work. Founder of Philadelphia Area UNICEF.[#] BmC-A.[4]

ESTAUGH, Elizabeth Haddon (1680–1762). Colonial proprietor, known as founder of Haddonfield, N. J. NjGbS, PHC. Bib.

ESTE, Charlotte (1761–1801). Revolutionary War spy and relief worker.[1]

*ESTE, Florence (1859–1926). Artist.[1]

*EUSTIS, Dorothy Leib Harrison Wood (1886–1946). Philanthropist, founder of The Seeing Eye, to train dogs for the blind.

EVE, Sarah (ca. 1750–1774). Diarist, artist. Bib.[1]

*EYTINGE, Rose (1835–1911). Actress. Bib.

F

FALCONER, Martha Platt (1862–1941). Social worker.

FARQUHARSON, Martha. See FINLEY, Martha.

FAUSET, Crystal Dreda Byrd (1893–1965). Black race relations specialist, state legislator, educator. PPAmF, PPAmP. (v. 4).

FAUSET, Jessie Redmon (1882–1961). Black writer and lecturer. Bib.[5]

FENTON, Beatrice (b. 1887). Sculptor. PPPCl.[4]

*FERGUSON, Elizabeth Graeme (1737–1801). Philadelphia litterateur. PHi, PPL. Bib.

FERRIS, Anna M. (1815–1890). Charity organizer. DeHi.[4]

FIELDE, Adele Marion (1839–1916). Entomologist, missionary, suffragist. PPAN.[4]

FINLEY, Martha (1828–1909). Author.

FISHER, Elizabeth Wilson (1873–1938). Civic leader.[1]

*FLEETWOOD, Sarah L. Iredell (b. 1851). Black educator, society leader.[5]

FLEISHER, Elizabeth R. Hirsh (1892–1975). Architect, designer of Parkway House, Philadelphia. PPA.[4]

*FLEISHER, Helen (1875–1931). Civic leader.[1]

*FORCE, Juliana Rieser (1876–1948). Art museum director. Bucks Cty. Free Lib.

FORESTIER, Auber. See MOORE, Annie Aubertine Woodward.

FORTEN, Charlotte L. See GRIMKÉ, Charlotte L. Forten.

FOURNIER, Mother Saint John (1814–1875). Roman Catholic nun, founder of Sisters of St. Joseph in Philadelphia. PPSSJ.[4]

FRANKLIN, Deborah Read (ca. 1707–1774). Wife of Benjamin Franklin. PPAmP. Bib.

*FRANKS, Rebecca (1760–1823). Philadelphia Tory belle of the Revolutionary period. PHi.

FREEMAN, Corinne Keen (1868–1932). Civic leader, World War I relief worker. PHi.[4]

FULD, Carrie Bamberger Frank (1864–1944). Philanthropist, co-founder of Institute for Advanced Study, Princeton.

*FULLER, Meta Vaux Warrick (1877–1968). Black sculptor. (v. 4).

FURNESS, Helen Kate Rogers (1837–1883). Shakespeare scholar.[4]

G

GAGAN, Elizabeth. See GAGAN, Mother Mary Gregory.

GAGAN, Mother Mary Gregory (1871–1960). Roman Catholic nun, social welfare and religious worker, administrator. PElDS.[4]

GAGE, Frances Dana Barker (1808–1884). Reformer, lecturer, author.

*GARRETT, Emma (ca. 1846–1893). Educator of the deaf.

GARRETT, Mary Elizabeth (1854–1915). Philanthropist. Bib.

*GARRETT, Mary Smith (1839–1925). Educator of the deaf, child welfare worker.

*GARRISON, Lucy McKim (1842–1877). Musician, collector of slave songs.

GEORGE, Mary. See OLDMIXON, Lady Mary.

GEROULD, Katharine Elizabeth Fullerton (1879–1944). Short story writer, essayist, novelist. NjP.

*GIBBONS, Abigail Hopper (1801–1893). Antislavery and prison reformer, Civil War nurse, welfare worker. Bib.

GILDER, Jeannette Leonard (1849–1916). Literary editor, critic, author.

*GILLESPIE, Elizabeth Duane (1821–1901). Civic leader, organizer of Sanitary Fair and Centennial Women's Committee. Bib.[1]

GODDARD, Mary Katherine (1738–1816). Printer of Declaration of Independence authorized by Congress, newspaper publisher, postmaster of Baltimore. PHi.

GODDARD, Sarah Updike (ca. 1700–1770). Printer.

GOLDMAN, Hetty (1881–1972). Archaeologist. PBm-A. (v. 4).

GRAEME, Elizabeth. See FERGUSON, Elizabeth Graeme.

GRANT, Alice Eliza (1858–1930). Educator, Principal of Girls Seminary, Academy of the New Church. PBa.[4]

*GRATZ, Rebecca (1781–1869). Pioneer Jewish charitable worker and Sunday school founder, noted beauty, reputed prototype for the heroine of Scott's *Ivanhoe*. PHi, PPJA, PPMAJ. Bib.

GRAY, Martha Ibbetson (1734–1799). Nurse, benefactor to Walnut St. prisoners during the Revolution.[1]

GREEN, Elizabeth Shippen (1871–1954). Illustrator, staff artist for *Harpers*. PChB, PP, PPPCl.[4]

GREENFIELD, Edna Kraus (d. 1949). Philanthropist. PHi.[4]

GREENFIELD, Elizabeth Taylor (1809–1876). Singer, known as "The Black Swan."

GREENWOOD, Grace. See LIPPINCOTT, Sara Jane Clarke.

GREW, Mary (1813–1896). Pennsylvania abolitionist, suffragist.

GRICE, Mary Van Meter (1860–1936). Leader in education, suffragist, pacifist, club-woman.[1]

*GRIFFITS, Hannah (1727–1817). Political poet. PHi, PPL.[4]

*GRIMKÉ, Charlotte L. Forten (1837–1914). Black teacher, author, Civil War educator of freedmen, diarist. Bib.

GRIMKÉ, Sarah Moore (1792–1873), and Angelina Emily (1805–1879). Abolitionists, women's rights pioneers. Bib.

GROSSMAN, Mary Foley (1903?–1972). Teacher, labor leader. PHC, PPT-U.[4]

GUMMERE, Amelia Mott (1859–1937). Quaker historian. PHC.[4]

GURNEY, Eliza Paul Kirkbride (1801–1881). Quaker minister. PHC, PHi. Bib.

H

HACKLEY, Emma Azalia Smith (1867–1922). Black singer and choir director.

HADDON, Elizabeth. See ESTAUGH, Elizabeth Haddon.

*HAHN, Dorothy Anna (1876–1950). Organic chemist.

*HAINES, Jane Bowne (1869–1937). Leader in horticulture.[1]

*HAINES, Margaret Vaux Wistar (1831–1917). Diarist. PPWy.[4]

HALE, Sarah Josepha Buell (1788–1879). Magazine editor. PPA. Bib.

HALL, Edith Hayward. See DOHAN, Edith Hayward Hall.

HALL, Sarah Ewing (1761–1830). Poet, critic.[1]

*HALLOWELL, Anna (1831–1905). Welfare worker, educational reformer, kindergarten leader.

*HALLOWELL, Sarah Catherine Fraley (1833–1914). Writer, suffragist, civic leader.[1]

*HANCOCK, Cornelia (1840–1927). Civil War nurse, educator of freedmen, charity worker, housing reformer. PHi, PSC-Hi. Bib.

HARCUM, Edith (1878–1958). Educator, founder of Harcum Jr. College. PBmH.[4]

HARDING, Charlotte. See BROWN, Charlotte Harding.

HARDING, Rebecca Blaine. See DAVIS, Rebecca Blaine Harding.

HARPER, Frances Ellen Watkins (1825–1911). Black lecturer, author, reformer.

HARRIS, Mary Belle (1874–1957). Prison administrator. Bib. (v. 4).

HARVEY, Ethel Browne (1885–1965). Cell biologist, embryologist. (v. 4).

HASSENCLEVER, Mary Melcher (b. before 1776). Revolutionary War relief worker.[1]

HATCHER, Orie Latham (1868–1946). English scholar, Southern pioneer in educational guidance.

HAVEN, Alice B. See HAVEN, Emily Bradley Neal.

HAVEN, Emily Bradley Neal (1827–1863). Author, magazine editor. Bib.

H.D. See DOOLITTLE, Hilda.

*HEACOCK, Annie (1838–1932). Teacher, abolitionist, suffragist.[1]

*HECKSCHER, Celeste de Longré Massey (1860–1928). Composer.[1]

*HENRY, Anne Wood (1732–1799). Treasurer of Lancaster County.[1]

HERBST, Josephine (1892–1969). Writer, journalist. (v. 4).

HEYGATE-HALL, Anne (1849–1936). Teacher, school administrator.[1]

HILL, Grace Livingston (1865–1947). Popular novelist. Bib.

HILL, Hannah Lloyd Delavall (1666–1726). Quaker preacher. Bib.[1]

HINCHMAN, Margaretta S. (1877–1954?). Illustrator, muralist, portraitist. PChB, PP, PPPCl.[4]

*HOGE, Jane Currie Blaikie (1811–1890). Civil War relief leader, Presbyterian church and welfare worker.

HOLSTEIN, Anna Morris (1824–1900). Civil War nurse, leader of patriotic societies. Bib.[1]

HOPE, Miriam (1845–1877). Diarist. NjGbS.[4]

HOWELL, Anna Blackwood (1769–1855). Manager of fisheries. NjWGHi.[4]

HOWLAND, Alice (1883–1968). Educator. PBmS.[4]

*HULL, Hannah Hallowell Clothier (1872–1958). Pacifist, suffragist. PSC-P. (v. 4).

HUNTER, Frances Tipton (d. 1957). Illustrator. PPPCl.[4]

*HUSBAND, Mary Morris (1820–1894). Civil War nurse.[1]

HUTTER, Elizabeth Shindel (1822–1895). Philanthropist, Civil War relief worker.[1]

I

*INGHAM, Mary Hall (1866–1937). Reformer, suffragist. PSC-Hi.

IRWIN, Agnes (1841–1914). Educator, first dean of Radcliffe College. PPT-R, PU-VS. Bib.

IRWIN, Sophia (ca. 1842–1915). Educator.[1]

J

JACKSON-COPPIN, Fanny. See COPPIN, Fanny Marion Jackson.

JACKSON, May Howard (1877–1931). Black sculptor.[5]

JACKSON, Rebecca Cox (1795–1871). Black Shaker elder. Bib.[4]

*JEANES, Anna Thomas (1822–1907). Philanthropist. PSC-Hi.

*JOHNSON, Emily Cooper (1885–1966). Quaker peace worker, author, editor, active in American Friends Service Committee. PSC-Hi.[4]

JOHNSON, Hattie O. Tanner (1863–1902). Black physician.[5]

JOHNSON, Rebecca Franks. See FRANKS, Rebecca.

JONES, Jane Elizabeth Hitchcock (1813–1896). Antislavery and women's rights lecturer.

*JONES, Rebecca (1739–1818). Quaker minister, educator, founder of feminist utopia. PHC, PSC-Hi. Bib.

JULIA, Sister. See MC GROARTY, Sister Julia.

JUNKIN, Margaret. See PRESTON, Margaret Junkin.

KATZENSTEIN, Caroline (ca. 1888–1968). Suffragist leader. PHi.[4]

KEASEY, Margaret Louise. See KEASEY, Mother Boniface.

KEASEY, Mother Boniface (1885–1931). Roman Catholic nun, founder of Missionary Servants of Most Blessed Trinity. PPMSBT.[4]

*KELLEY, Florence (1859–1932). Social reformer, long-time secretary of National Consumers' League. Bib.

KEMBLE, Frances Anne (1809–1893). Actress, author, abolitionist, known as Fanny Kemble. PHi, PPT-R. Bib.

KIERAN, Mother Mary John (1825–1888). Roman Catholic nun, Superior of Sisters of St. Joseph, educator. PPSSJ.[4]

KILGORE, Carrie Burnham (1838–1909). Teacher, lawyer, advocate of women's rights.

KING, Georgiana Goddard (1871–1939). Educator. PBm-A.[4]

KINGSBURY, Susan Myra (1870–1949). Social investigator, social work educator. PBm-A.

KIRKBRIDE, Eliza Butler (1836–1922). Civic leader, social welfare organizer.[1]

KITE, Mary (1792–1861). Quaker minister. PHC.[4]

KNOPF, Eleanora Frances Bliss (1883–1974). Geologist. (v. 4).

KROEGER, Alice Bertha (1864–1909). Librarian, library school director. PPD-L.

*KUGLER, Anna Sarah (1856–1930). Lutheran medical missionary to India. PPMCP.

KURYLAS, Sister Euphemia (1879–1963). Roman Catholic nun, founder of Sisters of St. Basil the Great in Philadelphia. PPOSBM.[4]

L

LANGEVICH, Mother Helen (1881–1916). Roman Catholic nun, founder of Sisters of St. Basil the Great in Philadelphia. PPOSBM.[4]

LANNEN, Mother Clement (1841–1910). Roman Catholic nun, Superior of Sisters of St. Joseph. PPSSJ.[4]

LARCOMBE, Jane Elizabeth (b. 1829). Author.[4]

LEA, Caroline Tyler Brown (d. 1930). Civic leader.[1]

*LEE, Jarena (b. 1783). Black AME minister, writer. PHi.[5]

*LEE, Mary Ann (1824?–1899). Ballerina, first American to dance "Giselle." PPCA.

LEONARD, Priscilla. See BISSELL, Emily Perkins.

LESLEY, Susan Lyman (1823–1904). Charity worker. PPAmP. Bib.[4]

*LESLIE, Eliza (1787–1858). Author, editor. Bib.

LEWIS, Florence A. (fl. 1890s). Black journalist, educator, social critic.[5]

*LEWIS, Graceanna (1821–1912). Natural scientist, artist, temperance worker, abolitionist.[+] PPAN, PSC-Hi. Bib.[1]

LINGELBACH, Anna Lane (1873–1954). Educator, women's rights advocate, clubwoman. PPT-CT.[4]

LIPPINCOTT, Alice (1846–1894). Civic leader, philanthropist. PHi.[4]

*LIPPINCOTT, Joanna Wharton (1858–1938). Civic leader.[1]

LIPPINCOTT, Sara Jane Clarke (1823–1904). Journalist, lecturer. NjP.

*LLOYD, Elizabeth (1848–1917). Teacher, writer, also known as Ruth Craydock.[1]

*LLOYD, Grace Growdon (1679–1760). Philanthropist.[1]

LLOYD, Hannah. See HILL, Hannah Lloyd Delavall.

*LOGAN, Celia (1837?–1904). Actress, journalist, novelist, playwright. (Listed under LOGAN, Olive.)

*LOGAN, Deborah Norris (1761–1839). Collector of historical records. PHi. Bib.

*LOGAN, Eliza (1829?–1872). Actress. (Listed under LOGAN, Olive.)

LONGACRE, Augusta McClintock (1843–1928). Historian.[1]

LONGSHORE, Hannah E. Myers (1819–1901). Pioneer woman physician. PPMCP. Bib.

*LONGSTRETH, Mary Anna (1811–1884). Educator. Bib.[1]

LORIMER, Alma Viola Ennis (1877?–1941). Civic leader, charitable worker.[#6]

LOVELL, Mary Frances (1844–1932). Humanitarian, philanthropist.[1]

LOWE-PORTER, Helen Tracy (1876–1963). Translator, writer. (v. 4).

LUCKIE, Mary Barton (1861–1964). Civic leader, suffragist, club-woman. PCDHi.[4]

*LUKENS, Rebecca Webb Pennock (1794–1854). Iron manufacturer. DeGE. Bib.

M

*MC CAULEY, Mary Ludwig Hays (1754?–1832). One of several women known as "Molly Pitcher", legendary heroine of the battle of Monmouth in the Revolutionary War. Bib.

*MC COLLIN, Frances (1892–1960). Composer. PP.[4]

*MAC DONALD, Jeanette (1903?–1965). Film actress, singer. Bib. (v. 4).

*MC DOWELL, Anne Elizabeth (1826–1901). Editor, journalist.

MAC DOWELL, Elizabeth (fl. 1880s). Painter. PPPAFA.[4]

MAC DOWELL, Susan. See EAKINS, Susan MacDowell.

MAC FARLANE, Catharine (1877–1969). Physician, founder of cancer detection clinic.[#] PPC, PPMCP.[4]

MC GROARTY, Sister Julia (1827–1901). Roman Catholic nun, educator.

*MACKLIN, Madge Thurlow (1893–1962). Physician, geneticist. (v. 4).

MADISON, Dolley Payne Todd (1768–1849). Washington hostess, wife of James Madison. NjP, PPINHP, PPPAFA. Bib.

MAPPS, Grace A. (ca. 1837–1891). Black educator, humanitarian.[5]

*MARKOE, Matilda Campbell (1849–1937). Episcopalian church worker, philanthropist.[1]

*MAROT, Helen (1865–1940). Social investigator, labor reformer, writer, editor.

*MARSHALL, Clara (1847–1931). Physician, Dean of the Women's Medical College of Pennsylvania. PPMCP, PWcHi.

*MARTIN, Elizabeth Price (1864–1932). Civic leader. PPPE.[1]

MASTERS, Sybilla (d. 1720). Inventor.

*MERRITT, Anna Lea (1844–1930). Artist.[1]

MERRY, Ann Brunton (1769–1808). Actress.

*MICHAEL, Helen Abbott (1857–1904). Chemist. PPAmP.[4]

MILLER, Frieda Segelke (1889–1973). State and federal official, labor reformer. (v. 4).

*MOORE, Annie Aubertine Woodward (1841–1929). Author, musician, translator.

MOORE, Caroline A. (1870?–1951). War relief worker.[#6]

*MOORE, Clara Sophia Jessup (1824–1899). Author, writer on etiquette. PHi.

MORAN, Mary Nimmo (1842–1899). Painter, etcher.

MORETON, Clara. See MOORE, Clara Sophia Jessup.

MORLEY, Christine (1880?–1970). Educator, historian. PCDHi.[4]

*MORRELL, Louise Bouvier Drexel (1863–1945). Philanthropist, advocate of education for blacks. PBeSBS.[4]

MORRIS, Elizabeth Carrington (1775–1865). Botanist. PPGHi.[4]

MORRIS, Lydia Ellicott (1872–1956). Philanthropist, founder of Charlotte Cushman Club.[4]

MORRIS, Margaretta Hare (1797–1867). Botanist. PPGHi.[4]

*MORRIS, Mary Wells (1764–1819). Pioneer.[1]

MORRIS, Susanna (1682–1755). Quaker minister. PHi.[4]

*MOSSELL, Gertrude Bustill (b. 1856). Black journalist, teacher, social critic.[5]

MOTT, Lucretia Coffin (1793–1880). Quaker minister, abolitionist, pioneer in the movement for women's rights. PSC-Hi. Bib.

MOULSON, Deborah (1801–1839). Educator.[1]

MUMFORD, Mary Eno Bassett (1842–1935). Philadelphia educational and civic leader, club-woman.

MYERS, Jane Viola (1831–1918). Pioneer woman physician. Bib.[4]

N

*NATT, Josephine Agnes (1862–1934). Educator.[1]

NEAL, Alice B. See HAVEN, Emily Bradley Neal.

NEALL, Adelaide W. (d. 1957). Author, editor. PHi.[4]

*NEILSON, Nellie (1873–1947). Historian.

NELSON, Alice Dunbar (1875–1935). Black author, teacher, social worker. Bib.

NICHOLS, Minerva Parker (1861–1949). Architect. PPA.

NUTT, Anna Rutter Savage (1686–1760). Owner of iron foundries.[2]

O

OAKLEY, Imogen Brashear (1854–1933). Civic leader.[1]

OAKLEY, Violet (1874–1960). Artist. PChB, PPD-M, PPFl, PPPCl. Bib.

*OBERHOLTZER, Sara Louisa (1841–1930). Promoter of school savings banks. PHi.[1]

OLDMIXON, Lady Mary (1768–1835). Actress.[4]

OSWALD, Elizabeth Holt (fl. 1795). Printer, publisher, editor.[3]

P

PAPEGOJA, Armegott Printz (ca. 1627–1695). Daughter of Gov. Printz and manager of Printz estates in New Sweden. PPAmS. Bib.[1]

PARK, Marion Edwards (1895–1960). Educator, president of Bryn Mawr College. PBm-A.[4]

PARRISH, Anne (1760–1800). Philanthropist, educator.[2]

PARRISH, Anne (1888–1954?). Author, illustrator. DeHi.[4]

PARRISH, Helen (1859–1942). Housing reformer, founder of Octavia Hill Association. PPT-U. Bib.[4]

PATTERSON, Mary Jane (1854–1894). Black educator. Bib.[5]

*PEALE, Anna Claypoole (1791–1878), Margaretta Angelica (1795–1882), Sarah Miriam (1800–1885). Painters of portraits and still lifes. PPPAFA. Bib.

PEART, Caroline (1870–1963). Portrait painter. PPPCl.[4]

PEASE, Mary Spenser (b. ca. 1810). Poet, author.[4]

PELL, Anna Johnson. See WHEELER, Anna Johnson Pell.

PEMBERTON, Caroline Hollingsworth (d. 1929). Author, socialist, civil rights advocate. Bib.[4]

PENN, Hannah Callowhill (1671–1726). Second wife and executrix of William Penn, acting proprietor of Pennsylvania. PHi, PSC-Hi. Bib.

*PENNELL, Elizabeth Robins (1855–1936). Author, art critic.

PENNINGTON, Mary Engle (1872–1952). Chemist, refrigeration specialist. (v. 4).

PERKINS, Frances (1880–1965). Social reformer, Secretary of Labor, first woman Cabinet member. Bib. (v. 4).

PETER, Sarah Anne Worthington King (1800–1877). Leader in charitable and Roman Catholic church work, founder of Philadelphia School of Design for Women (Moore College of Art). PPF, PPMo. Bib.

PITCHER, Molly. See MC CAULEY, Mary Ludwig Hays.

*PLEASANT, Mary Ellen (1814?–1904). Sometimes called "Mammy" Pleasant, California pioneer, boardinghouse keeper.

PORTER, Charlotte Endymion (1857–1942). Co-founder of "Poet Lore" magazine. PPT-R, PU-VS.

PORTER, Hannah Armstrong (1860–1958). Leader of Red Cross Volunteers. DeHi.[4]

PORTER, Helen Tracy Lowe. See LOWE-PORTER, Helen Tracy.

POTTER, Ellen Culver (1871–1958). Physician, specialist in preventive medicine. PPMCP.[4]

*POWDERMAKER, Hortense (1896–1970). Anthropologist. (v. 4).

POWERS, Nora (1799?–1865). Philadelphia dun and street character, known as "Crazy Nora." PHi.[4]

PRATT, Anna Beach (1867–1932). Social worker.

*PRESTON, Ann (1813–1872). Physician, dean of the Female (Women's) Medical College of Pennsylvania. PPMCP.

*PRESTON, Margaret Junkin (1820–1897). Southern poet. Bib.

*PRICE, Rachel Kirk (1763–1847). Quaker minister.[1]

PRINTZ, Armegott. See PAPEGOJA, Armegott Printz.

PRINTZ, Maria von Linnestau (early 1600s). Wife of Johan Bjornsson Printz, first Governor of New Sweden.[1]

PUGH, Sarah (1800–1884). Teacher, abolitionist, woman's suffragist.

PURVIS, Harriet Forten (fl. 1860s). Black abolitionist, worker on Underground Railroad.[5]

Q

QUINTON, Amelia Stone (1833–1926). Organizer of Indian reform.

R

RALLS, Elizabeth (b. ca. 1800). Black humanitarian.[5]

RAMBAUT, Mary Lucinda Bonney. See BONNEY, Mary Lucinda.

RAND, Marie Gertrude (1886–1970). Experimental psychologist. (v. 4).

RECKLESS, Hester (1776–1881). Black abolitionist, Underground Railroad worker.[5]

REED, Esther De Berdt (1746–1780). Leader of women's relief work during the American Revolution. Bib.

REILLY, Marion (1879–1928). Mathematician, Dean of Bryn Mawr College. PBm-A.[1]

*REPPLIER, Agnes (1855–1950). Essayist. NjP, PRosI, PU-VS. Bib.

RICHARDS, Linda (1841–1930). Pioneer nursing educator. Bib.

RICHMOND, Mary Ellen (1861–1928). Social worker.

RIPPIN, Jane Parker Deeter (1882–1953). Social worker, Girl Scout executive, journalist. (v. 4).

ROBINSON, Hannah (1803–1878). Jeweler, silversmith. DeHi.[4]

*RORER, Sarah Tyson Heston (1849–1937). Teacher of cooking, cookbook author, dietician. Bib.

ROSEHILL, Lady Margaret Cheer (18th cent.). Actress.[2]

*ROSS, Betsy (1752–1836). Legendary maker of the first Stars and Stripes, proprietor of upholstery factory. Bib.

ROWSON, Susanna Haswell (1762–1824). Author, poet, playwright, actress. PU-VS. Bib.[4]

*RUSH, Ann Ridgway (1799–1857). Society leader. PPL.[1]

RUSHMORE, Jane P. (1864–1958). Pioneer social and peace worker, first woman clerk of Philadelphia Yearly Meeting. Bib.[4]

S

SAMAROFF, Olga (1882–1948). Concert pianist, teacher. Bib.

SANFORD, Maria Louise (1836–1920). Teacher, college professor. Bib.

SANFORD, Weltha L. (1828–1916). Educator.[1]

*SARTAIN, Emily (1841–1927). Painter, mezzotint engraver, art educator. PHi, PPMo, PPPAFA, PPPCl.

SARTAIN, Harriet (1873–1957). Engraver, painter, art educator. PPMo.[4]

SARTAIN, Harriet Amelia Judd (1830–1923). Physician, promoter of homeopathic medicine and women's rights.[1]

SAUNDERS, Hetty (d. 1862). Black poet.[5]

*SCHOFF, Hannah Kent (1853–1940). Child welfare worker, juvenile court reformer.

*SCHOFIELD, Martha (1839–1916). Educator of freedmen. PSC-Hi. Bib.

SCOTT, Charlotte Angas (1858–1931). Mathematician.

SEILER, Emma Diruff (1821–1886). Voice and elocution teacher, scientist.[+] PPAmP. Bib.[4]

SHADD, Mary Ann. See CARY, Mary Ann Shadd.

SHAW, Anna Howard (1847–1919). First woman Methodist minister, lecturer, suffragist. PCDHi. Bib.

*SHELTON, Matilda Hart (1846–1894). Civic leader.[1]

SHIPLEY, Elizabeth Anthony (1859–1929), Hannah Taylor (1850–1932), Katherine Morris (1868–1929). Educators, founders of Shipley School. PBmS.[4]

*SHIPLEY, Miriam Allen De Ford (1888–1975). Writer. PPT-CT.[4]

SIMPSON, Ellen Holmes Verner (pre 1837–1897). Civic leader, charity organizer.[1]

SMITH, Bessie (1894–1937). Black blues singer.

*SMITH, Elizabeth Drexel (1855–1890). Philanthropist. PBeSBS.[4]

SMITH, Georgine Wetherill (d. 1954). Artist, all media. PPPCl.[4]

*SMITH, Hannah Whitall (1832–1911). Religious author, evangelist, feminist, temperance reformer. Bib.

*SMITH, Jessie Willcox (1863–1935). Painter, illustrator. PChB, PPPAFA, PPPCl. Bib.

SMITH, Kate Douglas. See WIGGIN, Kate Douglas Smith.

*SMITH, Margaret Bayard (1778–1844). Author, early chronicler of Washington society.

*SMITH, Mary (1842–1878). Painter. PPPAFA.[4]

*SMITH, Mary Rebecca Darby (1814–1886). Bibliophile. PPL.[4]

SMITH, Nora Archibald. See WIGGIN, Kate Douglas Smith.

SMITH, Wuanita (1866–1959). Illustrator, etcher, printmaker, miniaturist. PPPCl.[4]

SPOFFORD, Grace Harriet (1887–1974). Music educator, administrator. (v. 4).

STANLEY, Elizabeth. See STANLEY, Sister Mary Raphael.

STANLEY, Sister Mary Raphael (1888–1975). Roman Catholic nun, educator, administrator. PElDS.[4]

*STEPHENS, Alice Barber (1858–1932). Illustrator, wood engraver for Scribners. PChB, PPPCl.[4]

STEVENS, Nettie Maria (1861–1912). Biologist, geneticist.

*STEVENSON, Christine Wetherill (1878–1922). Art and theatre patron.[1]

STEVENSON, Sara Yorke (1847–1921). Civic leader, archaeologist, club-woman.[+] Bib.[1]

STILLWELL, Mary H. (1872–1933). Dentist, first president of Women's Dental Association. PHi.[4]

STOCKTON, Louise (1838–1914). Author.[4]

STOKOWSKI, Olga Samaroff. See SAMAROFF, Olga.

STUART, Jessie Bonstelle. See BONSTELLE, Jessie.

SULLY, Jane Cooper (1807–1877). Painter. PPPAFA.[4]

SWINDLER, Mary Hamilton (1884–1967). Archaeologist, classicist. (v. 4).

T

TAFT, Jessie (1882–1960). Psychologist, social work educator. Bib. (v. 4).

TANNER, Juliet L. (1833–1909). Artist, watercolorist. PWRHi.[4]

TAPPAN, Eva March (1854–1930). Teacher, author of children's books.

TAYLOR, Lily Ross (1886–1969). Classicist. PBm-A. (v. 4).

THOMAS, Martha Carey (1857–1935). Educator, feminist, first president of Bryn Mawr College, founder of Bryn Mawr Summer School. PBm-A, PPAmP. Bib.

*THOMAS, Mary Frame Myers (1816–1888). Physician, suffragist.

TIMOCHKO, Sister Paphnutia (1879–1963). Roman Catholic nun, founder of Sisters of St. Basil the Great in Philadelphia. PPOSBM.[4]

TOWNSEND, Mira Sharpless (1787–1858). Author, abolitionist.[1]

TRACY, Martha (1876–1942). Physician, Dean of Women's Medical College of Pennsylvania, health administrator. PPMCP.

TREAT, Mary Adelia Davis (1830–1923). Natural scientist. NjVHi. Bib.[4]

*TURNER, Eliza L. Sproat Randolph (1826–1903). Author, suffragist, women's club leader. PHi.

TUTHILL, Louisa Caroline Huggins (1799–1879). Author. PPA.

V

VENNING, Louise Julia (b. ca. 1864). Black educator, musician.[5]

*VERNON, Elizabeth Cooper (1833–1865). Civil War drill master.[1]

*VERNON, Mabel (1883–1975). Suffragist, feminist, pacifist. PSC-P. (v. 4).

W

WADE, Lydia Evans (1646–1701). Colonial philanthropist.[1]

*WALCOTT, Mary Morris Vaux (1860–1940). Artist, naturalist.

WALDRON, Anna. See WALDRON, Mother Mary Patricia.

WALDRON, Mother Mary Patricia (1834–1916). Roman Catholic nun, founder of Religious Sisters of Mercy in Philadelphia. PMeRSM.[4]

WARD, Mrs. H. O. See MOORE, Clara Sophia Jessup.

WARING, Laura Wheeler (1887–1948). Black portrait painter, educator.[5]

WARNER, Emalea Pusey (1853–1948). Civic leader. DeHi.[4]

WARREN, Ann Brunton. See MERRY, Ann Brunton.

WASHINGTON, Martha Dandridge Custis (1731–1802). Wife of George Washington.

WATKINS, Frances Ellen. See HARPER, Frances Ellen Watkins.

WATSON, Margaret (before 1683). Only person tried for witchcraft in Pennsylvania; she was acquitted.[1]

WEBER, Sarah S. Stilwell (1878–1939). Illustrator, especially of children's stories. PChB, PPPCl.[4]

WEIL, Mathilde (fl. 1890s). Photographer. PPPCl.[4]

WENZELL, Charlotte Este. See ESTE, Charlotte.[1]

WHARTON, Anne Hollingsworth (1845–1928). Author. PHi.[1]

*WHARTON, Deborah Fisher (1795–1888). Philanthropist.[1]

WHARTON, Susanna Parrish (1852–1928). Social reformer. PSC-P.[4]

WHEELER, Anna Johnson Pell (1883–1966). Mathematician. PBm-A. (v. 4).

*WHITE, Caroline Earle (1833–1916). Humane society organizer.[1]

*WIGGIN, Kate Douglas Smith (1856–1923). Author, kindergarten educator.

WIGNELL, Ann Brunton. See MERRY, Ann Brunton.

WILKINS, Amy Draper (b. pre 1776). Revolutionary War patriot.[1]

*WILKINSON, Ann Biddle (1757–1807). Pioneer.[1]

WILSON, Ellen Louise Axson (1860–1914). First wife of Woodrow Wilson, twenty-eighth president of the United States. NjR-AL.

WILSTACH, Anna H. (1816?–1892). Philanthropist, art patron. PPPM.[4]

WISCHNEWETZKY, Florence Kelley. See KELLEY, Florence.

WISTER, Frances Anne (1875?–1956). Civic leader, founder of Women's Committee for the Philadelphia Orchestra.[#][6]

*WISTER, Mary Channing Wister (1870–1918). Humanitarian.[1]

*WISTER, Sally (1761–1804). Diarist, writer. NjR-AL, PHi. Bib.[1]

WITTENMYER, Annie Turner (1827–1900). Civil War relief worker, leader in Methodist church and charitable work, first president of the Women's Christian Temperance Union.

*WOODBRIDGE, Louise Deshong (1848–1925). Civic leader, club-woman.[1]

WOODWARD-MOORE, Annie Aubertine. See MOORE, Annie Aubertine Woodward.

*WOOLMAN, Mary Raphael Schenck (1860–1940). Home economist, textile specialist, vocational educator.

WORRELL, Emma (1834–1931). Civic leader. DeHi.[4]

*WRIGHT, Patience Lovell (1725–1786). Sculptor in wax. NjBHi. Bib.

WRIGHT, Susanna (1697–1784). Colonial frontierswoman and poet. PHi, PPL.

Z

ZIMBALIST, Mary Louise Curtis Bok (1876–1970). Music patron, philanthropist.[#] PHi, PPCl. (v. 4).

Bryn Mawr College Students (Bryn Mawr College Archives Photograph Collection)

Bibliography

This bibliography is designed to focus particularly on the Delaware Valley area and to relate to the section on notable women. It is suggestive rather than comprehensive; bibliographies in the listed works should be consulted for further information.

Some major histories of the area have been included to provide the local setting; a selection of general source books and works on aspects of women's history are listed to provide the national context of the field. For the most part the rest are directly related to or touch on women's history of the geographical area defined. With the exception of autobiographical material, the published works of women listed in the notable section have not been included since they tend to be more readily accessible through library catalogues and other finding aids.

Some works on women not listed among the notables are included—diaries of matrons that shed light on women's lives, and a biography of Alice Paul, whose importance is undoubted, but whose longevity kept her off the list.

BIBLIOGRAPHIES AND SOURCE WORKS

Cantor, Aviva, comp. *The Jewish Woman, 1900–1980: A Bibliography.* New York, 1981.

Davis, Leonard G. *The Black Woman in American Society: A Selected Annotated Bibliography.* Boston, 1975.

Harrison, Cynthia E., ed. *Women in American History A Bibliography.* Santa Barbara, Calif., 1979.

Herstory. Microfilm of International Women's History Periodical Archives. Berkeley, Calif.

Hinding, Andrea, ed. *Women's History Sources: A Guide to Archives and Manuscript Collections in the United States.* 2 vols. New York, 1979.

Kelly-Gadol, Joan. *Women's History: A Critically Selected Bibliography.* 4th ed. Bronxville, N.Y., 1976.

Krichmar, Albert. *Women's Rights Movement in the United States 1848–1970; A Bibliography and Sourcebook.* Metuchen, N.J., 1972.

Leonard, Eugenie A., et al. *The American Woman in Colonial and Revolutionary Times, 1565–1800; A Syllabus with Bibliography.* Philadelphia, 1962.

Lerner, Gerda. *Bibliography in the History of American Women.* 3d rev. ed. Bronx-
ville, N.Y., 1978.
Resource Guide 6 Women and Women's Issues. Free Library of Philadelphia. Phila-
delphia, 1981.
Steiner-Scott, Elizabeth, and Elizabeth Pearce Wagle. *New Jersey Women, 1770–
1970: A Bibliography.* Rutherford, N.J., 1978.
Stineman, Esther. *Women's Studies: A Recommended Core Bibliography.* Littleton,
Colo., 1979.

BIOGRAPHY—GENERAL

Barlow, Marjorie Dana, ed. *Notes on Woman Printers in Colonial America and the
U.S. 1639–1975.* Charlottesville, Va., 1976.
Biddle, Gertrude B., and Sarah D. Lowrie, eds. *Notable Women of Pennsylvania.*
Philadelphia, 1942.
Biographical Cyclopedia of American Women. 2 vols. New York, 1924–1928.
Bolton, Sarah Elizabeth Mary. *Famous Leaders Among Women.* New York, 1895.
———. *Famous Types of Womanhood.* New York, ca. 1892.
———. *Lives of Girls Who Became Famous.* 6th rev. ed. New York, 1941.
———. *Successful Women.* Boston, 1888.
Bradford, Gamaliel. *Portraits of American Women.* Boston, 1917–1918.
Brown, Hallie Q. *Homespun Heroines and Other Women of Distinction.* Xenia,
Ohio, 1926.
Collins, Jim, and Glenn B. Opitz. *Women Artists in America.* Rev. ed. Poughkeepsie,
N.Y., 1980.
Dexter, Elizabeth A. *Career Women of America, 1776–1840.* Francestown, N.H.,
1950.
———. *Colonial Women of Affairs.* Boston, 1924.
Ellet, Elizabeth F. *Women of the American Revolution.* 3 vols. New York, 1856.
Eminent Women of the Age. 2d ed. Hartford, 1872.
Griswold, Rufus Wilmot, ed. *The Female Poets of America.* 2d ed. Philadelphia,
1859.
———. *Gems from American Female Poets, with Brief Biographical Notices.* 3d ed.
Philadelphia, 1844.
Hale, Sarah Josepha. *Woman's Record; or, Sketches of All Distinguished Women,
from "the Beginning" till A.D. 1850.* 3d ed. New York, 1870.
Halsey, Francis Whiting, ed. *Women Authors of Our Day in Their Homes.* New York,
1903.
Hanaford, Phebe A. *Daughters of America.* Augusta, Me., 1882.
Hart, John S. *The Female Prose Writers of America.* Philadelphia, 1855.
Howes, Durward, ed. *American Women, 1935–1940: A Composite Biographical
Dictionary.* Reprint. 2 vols. Detroit, 1981.
Hudak, Leona M. *Early American Women Printers and Publishers 1639–1820.*
Metuchen, N.J., 1978.
James, Edward T., ed. *Notable American Women: 1607–1950; A Biographical
Dictionary.* 3 vols. Cambridge, Mass., 1971.
Majors, Monroe Alphus. *Noted Negro Women, Their Triumphs and Activities.* Chicago,
1893.
Mead, Mrs. Kate Campbell. *Medical Women of America; a Short History of the
Pioneer Medical Women of America.* New York, 1933.

Mossell, Mrs. N.F. *Afro-American Women*. Philadelphia, 1918.

Rawle, William Brooke. "Laurel Hill and Some Colonial Dames Who Once Lived There." *Pennsylvania Magazine* 35 (1911): 385–414.

Sicherman, Barbara, and Carol Hurd Green, eds. *Notable American Women: The Modern Period: A Biographical Dictionary*. Cambridge, Mass., 1980.

Willard, Frances E., and Mary A. Livermore, eds. *A Woman of the Century*. Buffalo, 1893.

Wister, Mrs. Sarah. *Worthy Women of Our First Century*. Philadelphia, 1877.

Yost, Edna. *American Women of Science*. Philadelphia, 1943.

BIOGRAPHY—INDIVIDUAL WOMEN

Alcott, Louisa May

Saxton, Martha. *Louisa May: A Modern Biography of Louisa May Alcott*. New York, 1977.

Stern, Madeleine B. *Louisa May Alcott*. Norman, Okla., 1950.

Aubrey, Martha

Vaux, George. "Rees Thomas and Martha Aubrey: Early Settlers in Merion." *Pennsylvania Magazine* 13 (1889): 292–97.

Barrymore, Ethel

Alpert, Hollis. *The Barrymores*. New York, 1964.

Barrymore, Ethel. *Memories, An Autobiography*. New York, 1955.

Bauduy, Victorine du Pont

Johnson, Mary. "Victorine du Pont: Heiress to the Educational Dream of Pierre Samuel du Pont de Nemours." *Delaware History* 19 (1980): 88–105.

Beaux, Cecilia

Beaux, Cecilia. *Background with Figures; Autobiography*. Boston, 1930.

Pennsylvania Academy of the Fine Arts. *The Paintings and Drawings of Cecilia Beaux*. Philadelphia, 1955.

Bingham, Anne Willing

Alberts, Robert C. *The Golden Voyage The Life and Times of William Bingham 1752–1804*. Boston, 1969.

Brown, Margaret L. "Mr. and Mrs. William Bingham of Philadelphia." *Pennsylvania Magazine* 61 (1937): 286–324.

Blackwell, Elizabeth

Ross, Ishbel. *Child of Destiny: The Life of Elizabeth Blackwell.* New York, 1949.

Sahli, Nancy. "A Stick to Break Our Heads With: Elizabeth Blackwell and Philadelphia Medicine." *Pennsylvania History* 44 (1977): 335–47.

Blankenburg, Lucretia Longshore

Blankenburg, Lucretia M. *The Blankenburgs of Philadelphia.* Chicago, 1928.

Bloor, Ella Reeve

Bloor, Ella Reeve. *We Are Many; An Autobiography.* New York, 1940.

Brewster, Anne Hampton

Fisher, Estelle. *A Gentle Journalist Abroad: The Papers of Anne Hampton Brewster
in the Library Company of Philadelphia.* Research Bulletin of the Free Library
of Philadelphia. Philadelphia, 1947.

Brown, Charlotte Harding

Brown, Ann Barton. *Charlotte Harding An Illustrator in Philadelphia.* Exhibition
Catalogue, Brandywine River Museum. Chadds Ford, Pa., 1982.

Buck, Pearl

Harris, Theodore F. *Pearl S. Buck, A Biography.* 2 vols. Binghamton, N.Y., 1969.

Cary, Mary Ann Shadd

Hancock, Harold B. "Mary Ann Shadd: Negro Editor, Educator, and Lawyer." *Delaware History* 15 (1973): 187–94.

Cassatt, Mary

Sweet, Frederick A. *Miss Mary Cassatt, Impressionist from Pennsylvania.* Norman,
Okla., 1966.

Chandler, Elizabeth Margaret

Lundy, Benjamin, *Memoir of the Life and Character of Elizabeth Margaret Chandler.*
Philadelphia, 1845.

Connelly, Cornelia Augusta

Bisgood, Marie Thérèse. *Cornelia Connelly: A Study in Fidelity.* Westminster, Md.,
1963.

Coppin, Fanny Marion Jackson

Perkins, Linda Maria. "Heed Life's Demand: The Educational Philosophy of Fanny Jackson Coppin." *Journal of Negro Education* 51 (1982): 181–90.

Corbin, Margaret Cochran

Hall, Edward Hagaman. *Margaret Corbin, Heroine of the Battle of Fort Washington, 16 November 1776.* New York, 1932.

Darragh, Lydia Barrington

Darrach, Henry. "Lydia Darragh of the Revolution." *Pennsylvania Magazine* 23 (1899): 86–91.

Davis, Rebecca Blaine Harding

Davis, Rebecca Harding. *Life in the Iron Mills.* With a biographical interpretation by Tillie Olsen. New York, 1972.

Langford, Gerald. *The Richard Harding Davis Years; A Biography of a Mother and Son.* New York, 1961.

De Cleyre, Voltarine

Avrich, Paul. *An American Anarchist: The Life of Voltarine De Cleyre.* Princeton, 1978.

Delano, Jane Arminda

Gladwin, Mary E. *The Red Cross and Jane Arminda Delano.* Philadelphia, 1931.

Dickinson, Anna Elizabeth

Anderson, Judith. "Anna Dickinson, Antislavery Radical." *Pennsylvania History* 3 (1936): 147–63.

Chester, Giraud. *Embattled Maiden; the Life of Anna Dickinson.* New York, 1951.

Young, James Harvey. "Anna Dickinson, Mark Twain, and Bret Harte." *Pennsylvania Magazine of History and Biography* 76 (1952): 39–46.

Drexel, Mother Mary Katharine

Duffy, Consuela Marie. *Katharine Drexel: A Biography.* Philadelphia, 1966.

Drinker, Elizabeth Sandwith

Crane, Elaine F. "The World of Elizabeth Drinker." *Pennsylvania Magazine of History and Biography* 107 (1983): 3–28.

Radbill, Kenneth A. "The Ordeal of Elizabeth Drinker." *Pennsylvania History* 47 (1980): 147–72.

Eakins, Susan MacDowell

Pennsylvania Academy of the Fine Arts. *Susan MacDowell Eakins, 1851–1938.*
Exhibition catalogue. Philadelphia, 1973.

Estaugh, Elizabeth Haddon

Clement, John. "Elizabeth Estaugh and Some of Her Contemporaries." *New Jersey
Historical Society Proceedings* 30 (1912–1913): 103–5.
Haddon, Elizabeth. *A True Narrative of the Early Settlement of New Jersey.* Philadel-
phia, 1898.

Eytinge, Rose

Eytinge, Rose. *Memories of Rose Eytinge.* New York, 1905.

Fauset, Jessie Redmon

Sylvander, Carolyn W. *Jessie Redmon Fauset: Black American Writer.* Troy, N.Y., 1980.

Ferguson, Elizabeth Graeme

Gratz, Simon. "Some Material for a Biography of Mrs. Elizabeth Fergusson, Née
Graeme." *Pennsylvania Magazine* 39 (1915): 257–321, 385–409; 41 (1917):
385–98.

Fisher, Sarah Logan

Wainwright, Nicholas B. " 'A Diary of Trifling Occurrences:' Philadelphia, 1776–
1778." *Pennsylvania Magazine of History and Biography* 82 (1958): 411–65.

Franklin, Deborah Read

Franklin, Benjamin. *The Autobiography of Benjamin Franklin,* ed. Leonard W. Lara-
bee. New Haven, 1964.

Frazer, Mrs.

Slaymaker, Samuel R. II. "Mrs. Frazer's Philadelphia Campaign." *Journal of the
Lancaster County Historical Society* 73 (1969): 185–209.

Garrett, Mary Elizabeth

Harper, Ida H. *The Life and Work of Susan B. Anthony.* 3 vols. Indianapolis, 1898–
1908.

Gibbons, Abigail Hopper

Emerson, Sarah Hopper, ed. *Life of Abby Hopper Gibbons, Told Chiefly through Her
Correspondence.* 2 vols. Putnam, N.Y., 1896–1897.

Gillespie, Elizabeth Duane

Gillespie, Elizabeth D. *A Book of Remembrance*. Philadelphia, 1901.

Gratz, Rebecca

Osterweis, Rollin Gustav. *Rebecca Gratz; A Study in Charm*. New York, 1935.

Grimké, Sarah Moore and Angelina Emily

Barnes, Gilbert, and D. L. Dumond, eds. *Letters of Theodore Dwight Weld, Angelina Grimké Weld and Sarah Grimké, 1822–1844*. New York, 1970.
Lerner, Gerda. *The Grimké Sisters from South Carolina*. Boston, 1967.
Lumpkin, Katharine Dupre. *The Emancipation of Angelina Grimké*. Chapel Hill, 1974.
Murphy, Carol. "Two Desegregated Hearts." *Quaker History* 53 (1964): 87–92.

Hale, Sarah Josepha Buell

Entrikin, Isabelle W. *Sarah Josepha Hale and "Godey's Lady's Book."* Philadelphia, 1946.
Finley, Ruth E. *The Lady of Godey's, Sarah Josepha Hale*. Philadelphia, 1931.

Harris, Mary Belle

Harris, Mary Belle. *I Knew Them in Prison*. New York, 1942.

Haven, Emily Bradley Neal

Richards, Mrs. Cornelia Holroyd. *Cousin Alice: A Memoir of Alice B. Haven*. 2d ed. New York, 1868.

Hill, Grace Livingston

Karr, Jean. *Grace Livingston Hill, Her Story and Her Writings*. New York, 1948.

Hill, Hannah Lloyd Delavall

Thomas, Mrs. Anna Lloyd. *Nancy Lloyd, the Journal of a Quaker Pioneer*. New York, 1927.

Holstein, Anna Morris

Holstein, Mrs. Anna Morris. *Three Years in Field Hospitals of the Army of the Potomac*. Philadelphia, 1867.

Irwin, Agnes

Repplier, Agnes. *Agnes Irwin, A Biography*. Garden City, N.Y., 1935.

Jackson, Rebecca Cox

Williams, Richard E. *Called and Chosen: The Story of Rebecca Jackson and Her Philadelphia Shakers*. Metuchen, N.J., 1981.

Jones, Rebecca

Allinson, William J., comp. *Memorials of Rebecca Jones*. Philadelphia, 1849.

Keith, Dame Ann Morgan

Keith, Charles P. "The Wife and Children of Sir William Keith." *Pennsylvania Magazine* 56 (1932): 1–8.

Kelley, Florence

Blumberg, Dorothy R. *Florence Kelley; The Making of a Social Pioneer*. New York, 1966.
Goldmark, Josephine. *Impatient Crusader: Florence Kelley's Life Story*. Urbana, 1953.

Kemble, Frances Ann

"Butler v. Butler: A Divorce Case Incident." *Pennsylvania Magazine of History and Biography* 79 (1955): 101–8.
Driver, Leota S. *Fanny Kemble*. Chapel Hill, 1933.

Lesley, Susan Lyman

Ames, Mrs. Mary, ed. *Life and Letters of Peter and Susan Lesley*. 2 vols. New York, 1909.

Leslie, Eliza

Smith, Ophia D. "Charles and Eliza Leslie." *Pennsylvania Magazine of History and Biography* 74 (1950): 512–27.

Lewis, Graceanna

Warner, Deborah Jean. *Graceanna Lewis, Scientist and Humanitarian*. Washington, D.C., 1979.

Logan, Deborah Norris

Premo, Terri L. " 'Like a Being Who Does Not Belong:' The Old Age of Deborah Norris Logan." *Pennsylvania Magazine of History and Biography* 107 (1983): 85–112.

Longshore, Hannah E. Myers. *See under Myers, Jane Viola.*

Longstreth, Mary Anna

Newlin, Margaret. *Memoir of Mary Anna Longstreth.* Philadelphia, 1886.

Lukens, Rebecca Webb Pennock

Wolcott, Robert W. *A Woman in Steel—Rebecca Lukens (1794–1854).* Princeton,
    1940.

McCauley, Mary Ludwig Hays

Perrine, William Davison. *Molly Pitcher of Monmouth County, N.J. and Captain
    Molly of Fort Washington, N.Y. 1778–1937.* (n.p.), 1937.
Smith, Samuel Steele. *A Molly Pitcher Chronology.* Monmouth Beach, N.J., 1972.

MacDonald, Jeanette

Stern, Lee Edward. *Jeanette MacDonald.* New York, 1977.

Madison, Dolley Payne Todd

Anthony, Katharine S. *Dolly Madison: Her Personal History and Her Era.* New York,
    1954.
Sifton, Paul G. " 'What a Dread Prospect. . .': Dolly Madison's Plague Year." *Pennsyl-
    vania Magazine of History and Biography* 87 (1963): 189–225.

Montour, Madame

Freeze, John G. "Madame Montour." *Pennsylvania Magazine* 3 (1879): 79–87.

Mott, Lucretia Coffin

Bacon, Margaret H. *Valiant Friend: The Life of Lucretia Mott.* New York, 1980.
Cromwell, Otelia. *Lucretia Mott.* Cambridge, Mass., 1958.
Greene, Dana. "Quaker Feminism: The Case of Lucretia Mott." *Pennsylvania History*
    48 (1981): 143–54.
Hollowell, Anna Davis. *James and Lucretia Mott: Life and Letters.* New York, 1884.
Rush, N. Orwin. "Lucretia Mott and the Philadelphia Antislavery Fairs." *Friends
    Historical Association Bulletin* 35 (1946): 69–75.
Williams, H. Justice. "Flight to the Suburbs." *Quaker History* 64 (1975): 105–9.

Myers, Jane Viola

Waite, Frederick Clayton. "The Three Myers Sisters—Pioneer Women Physicians."
    Medical Review of Reviews 39 (1933): 114–20.

Nelson, Alice Dunbar

Hull, Gloria T. "Alice Dunbar-Nelson: Delaware Writer and Woman of Affairs." *Dela-
    ware History* 17 (1976): 87–103.

Norris, Sarah

Parson, William T. "The Brief Married Life of Isaac and Sarah Norris." *Quaker History* 57 (1968): 67–83.

Oakley, Violet

"Violet Oakley." *Philadelphia Museum of Art Bulletin* 75 #325 (1979).

Papegoja, Armegott Printz

Sawyer, William E. "Governor Printz's Daughter and the Island of Tinicum." *Pennsylvania History* 25 (1958): 109–14.

Patterson, Mary Jane

Hutchinson, Louise D. *Anna J. Cooper: A Voice from the South.* Washington, D.C., 1981.

Paul, Alice

Stevens, Doris. *Jailed for Freedom.* New York, 1920.

Peale, Anna Claypoole, Margaretta Angelica, Sarah Miriam

Born, Wolfgang. "The Female Peales, Their Art and its Tradition." *American Collector* 15 (1946): 12–14.
Hunter, Wilbur H., and John Mahey. *Miss Sarah Miriam Peale, 1800–1885.* Exhibition catalogue, Peale Museum. Baltimore, 1967.

Pemberton, Caroline Hollingsworth

Foner, Philip. "Caroline Hollingsworth Pemberton: Philadelphia Socialist Champion of Black Equality." *Pennsylvania History* 43 (1976): 227–51.

Penn, Hannah Callowhill

Cadbury, Henry J. "Hannah Callowhill and Penn's Second Marriage." *Pennsylvania Magazine of History and Biography* 81 (1957): 76–82.
Drinker, Sophie H. *Hannah Penn and the Proprietorship of Pennsylvania.* Philadelphia, 1958.

Perkins, Frances

Martin, George W. *Madam Secretary, Frances Perkins.* Boston, 1976.
Mohr, Lillian Holmen. *Frances Perkins: "That Woman in FDR's Cabinet."* Croton-on-Hudson, N.Y. 1979.

Peter, Sarah Anne Worthington King

King, Margaret R. *Memoirs of the Life of Mrs. Sarah Peter.* 2 vols. Cincinnati, 1889.
McAllister, Anna Shannon. *In Winter We Flourish: Life and Letters of Sarah Worthington King Peter.* New York, 1939.

Preston, Margaret Junkin

Allan, Elizabeth Preston, comp. *The Life and Letters of Margaret Junkin Preston.*
Boston, 1903.

Reed, Esther De Berdt

Reed, William B. *Life of Esther de Berdt Afterwards Esther Reed of Pennsylvania.*
Philadelphia, 1853.

Repplier, Agnes

Lukacs, John A. *Philadelphia, Patricians and Philistines, 1900–1950.* New York,
1981.
Stokes, George S. *Agnes Repplier, Lady of Letters.* Philadelphia, 1949.
Witmer, Emma. *Agnes Repplier: A Memoir.* Philadelphia, 1957.

Richards, Linda

Richards, Linda Ann Judson. *Reminiscences of Linda Richards, America's First Trained
Nurse.* Boston, 1911.

Rorer, Sarah Tyson Heston

Weigley, Emma Seifrit. "The Philadelphia Chef: Mastering the Art of Philadelphia
Cookery." *Pennsylvania Magazine of History and Biography* 96 (1972):
229–40.

Ross, Betsy

Miller, William C. "The Betsy Ross Legend." *The Social Studies* 37 (1946): 317–23.
Parry, Edwin S. *Betsy Ross, Quaker Rebel.* Philadelphia, 1930.

Rowson, Susanna Haswell

Martin, Wendy. "Profile: Susanna Rowson, Early American Novelist." *Women's Stud-
ies* 2 (1974): 1–8.
Weil, Dorothy. *In Defense of Women: Susanna Rowson (1762–1824).* University
Park, Pa., 1976.

Rushmore, Jane P.

Johnson, Emily Cooper. *Under Quaker Appointment.* Philadelphia, 1953.

Samaroff, Olga

Samaroff Stokowski, Olga. *An American Musician's Story.* New York, 1939.

Sanford, Maria Louise

Whitney, Helen Ardell. *Maria Sanford.* Minneapolis, 1922.

Schofield, Martha

Patterson, Mary S. *Martha Schofield, Servant of the Least.* Wallingford, Pa., 1944.

Seiler, Emma Diruff

Scull, Marie Seiler (?). *The Life of My Mother.* Boston, 1902.

Shaw, Anna Howard

Linkugel, Wil A., and Kim Griffin. "The Distinguished War Service of Dr. Anna Howard Shaw." *Pennsylvania History* 28 (1961): 372–85.
Shaw, Anna Howard, with Elizabeth Jordan. *The Story of a Pioneer.* New York, 1915.

Smith, Hannah Whitall

Smith, Logan Pearsall. *Philadelphia Quaker.* New York, 1950.
Strachey, Barbara. *Remarkable Relations The Story of the Pearsall Smith Women.* New York, 1982.

Smith, Jessie Willcox

Catalogue to the Memorial Exhibition of the Work of Jessie Willcox Smith. Exhibition Catalogue, Pennsylvania Academy of the Fine Arts. Philadelphia, 1935.

Stevenson, Sara Yorke

Civic Club of Philadelphia. *Sara Yorke Stevenson.* Philadelphia, 1922.

Taft, Jessie

Taft, Julia J. *Jessie Taft: Therapist and Social Work Educator: A Professional Biography.* Edited by Virginia P. Robinson. Philadelphia, 1962.

Thomas, Martha Carey

Finch, Edith. *Carey Thomas of Bryn Mawr.* New York, 1947.

Thompson, Mary Wilson

Higgins, Anthony, ed. "Mary Wilson Thompson Memoir." *Delaware History* 18 (1978–79): 43–62, 126–51, 194–217, 238–66.

Treat, Mary Adelia Davis

Weiss, Harry B. "Mrs. Mary Treat, 1830–1923, Early New Jersey Naturalist." *Proceedings of the New Jersey Historical Society* 73 (1955): 258–73.

Tybout, Ella Middleton

Lancaster, Robert V. "Ella Middleton Tybout, Chronicler of the Delaware Scene." *Delaware History* 3 (1949): 155–70.

Waldron, Mother Mary Patricia

Mother Mary Patricia Waldron First Superior of the Sisters of Mercy (Dublin Foundation) in the Diocese of Philadelphia. (n.p.), 1916.

Wister, Sarah Butler

Wister, Fanny Kemble. "Sarah Butler Wister's Civil War Diary." *Pennsylvania Magazine of History and Biography* 102 (1978): 271–327.

Wright, Lydia

Rubincam, Milton. "Lydia Wright and Her Sisters the Quaker Maidens Who Defied the Stern Puritans." *Proceedings of the New Jersey Historical Society* 58 (1940): 103–18.

Wright, Patience Lovell

Long, J.C. "Patience Wright of Bordentown." *Proceedings of the New Jersey Historical Society* 79 (1961): 118–23.
Sellers, Charles Coleman. *Patience Wright, American Artist and Spy in George III's London.* Middletown, Conn., 1976.

BIOGRAPHY—JOURNALS AND LETTERS

Assheton, Susan

"Susan Assheton's Book." Ed. with a Preface by Joseph M. Beatty, Jr. *Pennsylvania Magazine* 55 (1931): 174–86.

Bradford, Phoebe George

W. Emerson Wilson, ed. "Phoebe George Bradford Diaries." *Delaware History* 16 (1974–1975): 1–21, 132–51, 244–67, 337–57.

Callender, Hannah

Vaux, George. "Extracts from the Diary of Hannah Callender." *Pennsylvania Magazine* 12 (1888): 432–56.

Cushman, Charlotte Saunders

Stebbins, Emma, ed. *Charlotte Cushman: Her Letters and Memories of Her Life.* Boston, 1878.

Drinker, Elizabeth Sandwith

Biddle, Henry D. *Extracts from the Journal of Elizabeth Sandwith Drinker from 1759 to 1807.* Philadelphia, 1889.

Eve, Sarah

Jones, Eva Eve. "Extracts from the Journal of Miss Sarah Eve (1772–73)." *Pennsylvania Magazine* 5 (1881): 19–36, 191–205.

Farmar, Eliza

Farmar, Eliza. "Letters of Eliza Farmar to Her Nephew." *Pennsylvania Magazine* 40 (1916): 199–207.

Galloway, Grace Growden

Werner, Raymond C. "Diary of Grace Growden Galloway, Kept at Philadelphia from June 17, 1778 to July 1, 1779." *Pennsylvania Magazine* 55 (1931): 32–94.
————. "Diary of Grace Growden Galloway, Kept at Philadelphia, July 1 to September 30, 1779." *Pennsylvania Magazine* 58 (1934): 152–89.

Grimké, Charlotte L. Forten

Billington, Ray Allen. *The Journal of Charlotte L. Forten.* New York, 1953.

Gurney, Eliza Paul Kirkbride

Mott, Richard P. *Memoir and Correspondence of Eliza P. Gurney.* Philadelphia, 1884.

Hancock, Cornelia

Hancock, Cornelia. *South After Gettysburg: Letters, 1863–1868.* New York, 1956.

Jackson, Rebecca Cox

Humez, Jean McMahon. *Gifts of Power: The Writings of Rebecca Jackson, Black Visionary, Shaker Eldress.* Amherst, Mass., 1981.

Kemble, Frances Anne

Ashby, Clifford. "Fanny Kemble's 'Vulgar Journal.'" *Pennsylvania Magazine of History and Biography* 98 (1974): 58–66.

Leach, Christiana

Hinckley, Robert H., ed. "Selections from the Diary of Christiana Leach of Kingsessing, 1765–1796." *Pennsylvania Magazine* 35 (1911): 343–50.

Morris, Margaret

Jackson, John W., ed. *Margaret Morris: Her Journal.* Philadelphia, 1949.

Mott, Lucretia Coffin

Tolles, Frederick B., ed. *Slavery and "The Woman Question"; Lucretia Mott's Diary of Her Visit to Great Britain to Attend the World's Anti-Slavery Convention of 1840.* Haverford, Pa., 1952.

Parrish, Helen

Davis, Allen F., and John F. Sutherland. "Reform and Uplift Among Philadelphia Negroes: The Diary of Helen Parrish, 1888." *Pennsylvania Magazine of History and Biography* 94 (1970): 496–517.

Pinzer, Maimie

Pinzer, Maimie. *The Maimie Papers.* Ed. Ruth Rosen. Old Westbury, N.Y., 1977.

Saltar, Fanny

Hoskins, E. B. "Fanny Saltar's Reminiscences of Colonial Days in Philadelphia." *Pennsylvania Magazine* 40 (1916): 187–98.

Shippen, Nancy

Armes, Ethel M., comp. *Nancy Shippen: Her Journal Book.* Philadelphia, 1935.

Smith, Hannah Whitall

Smith, Logan Pearsall, ed. *Philadelphia Quaker: The Letters of Hannah Whitall Smith.* New York, 1950.

Thomas, Martha Carey

Dobkin, Marjorie Housepian, ed. *The Making of a Feminist: Early Diaries and Journals of M. Carey Thomas.* Kent, Ohio, 1980.

Warder, Ann

Cadbury, Sarah. "Extracts from the Diary of Mrs. Ann Warder." *Pennsylvania Magazine* 17 (1893): 444–61, 18 (1894): 51–63.

Wister, Sally

Myers, Albert C., ed. *Sally Wister's Journal*. Philadelphia, 1902.
Wister, Sarah. *Journal . . . 1777–1787*. Philadelphia, 1902.

Wister, Sarah Butler

Wister, Fanny Kemble. "Sarah Butler Wister's Civil War Diary." *Pennsylvania Magazine of History and Biography* 102 (1978): 271–327.

HISTORY—GENERAL

Munroe, John A. *Colonial Delaware: A History*. Millwood, N.Y., 1979.
Pomfret, John E. *Colonial New Jersey; A History*. New York, 1973.
Scharf, J. Thomas. *History of Delaware, 1609–1888*. 2 vols. Philadelphia, 1888.
Scharf, J. Thomas, and Thompson Westcott. *History of Philadelphia*. 3 vols. Philadelphia, 1884.
Weigley, Russell F., ed. *Philadelphia: A 300-Year History*. New York, 1982.

HISTORY—TOPICAL

Alexander, John K. *Render Them Submissive: Responses to Poverty in Philadelphia, 1760–1800*. Amherst, 1980.
Bacon, Margaret H. "Friends and the 1876 Centennial." *Quaker History* 66 (1977): 41–50.
Baltzell, Edward Digby. *Philadelphia Gentlemen: The Making of a National Upper Class*. Philadelphia, 1979.
Benjamin, Philip. *Philadelphia Quakers in the Industrial Age, 1865–1920*. Philadelphia, 1976.
Benson, Adolph B., and Naboth Hedin, eds. *Swedes in America, 1638–1938*. New Haven, 1938.
Bittinger, Lucy F. *Germans in Colonial Times*. Philadelphia, 1901.
Blockson, Charles L. *Pennsylvania's Black History*. Philadelphia, 1975.
Bolton, Charles K. *Scotch-Irish Pioneers in Ulster and America*. Boston, 1910.
Bremner, Robert H., ed. *Children and Youth in America: A Documentary History, 1600–1932*. 2 vols. Cambridge, Mass., 1970.
Brown, Herbert R. *The Sentimental Novel in America, 1789–1860*. Durham, N.C., 1940.
Brown, Ira V. *Pennsylvania Reformers: From Penn to Pinchot*. University Park, Pa., 1966.
Burnston, Sharon Ann. "Babies in the Well: An Underground Insight into Deviant Behavior in Eighteenth-Century Philadelphia." *Pennsylvania Magazine of History and Biography* 106 (1982): 151–86.
Calhoun, Arthur W. *The Social History of the American Family from Colonial Times to the Present*. 3 vols. New York, 1917–1919.
Clark, Dennis. "The Adjustment of Irish Immigrants to Urban Life: The Philadelphia Experience, 1840–1897." Ph.D. thesis, Temple University, 1970.
———. "Babes in Bondage: Indentured Irish Children in Philadelphia in the Nine-

teenth Century." *Pennsylvania Magazine of History and Biography* 101 (1977): 475–86.

―――. *The Irish In Philadelphia; Ten Generations of Urban Experience,* Philadelphia, 1973.

―――. *The Irish Relations: Trials of an Immigrant Tradition.* Rutherford, N.J., 1982.

Davis, Allen Freeman, ed. *The Peoples of Philadelphia; A History of Ethnic Groups and Lower Class Life, 1790–1940.* Philadelphia, 1973.

Drinker, Cecil. *Not So Long Ago: A Chronicle of Medicine and Doctors in Colonial Philadelphia.* New York, 1937.

DuBois, W.E.B. *The Philadelphia Negro: A Social Study: Together with a Special Report on Domestic Service by Isabel Eaton.* Reprint. New York, 1967.

Freedman, Estelle B. *Their Sisters Keepers: Women's Prison Reform in America, 1830–1930.* Ann Arbor, 1981.

Golab, Carol A. "The Polish Communities of Philadelphia, 1870–1920: Immigrant Distribution and Adaptation in Urban America." Ph.D. thesis, University of Pennsylvania, 1971.

Haber, Carole. "The Old Folks at Home: The Development of Institutionalized Care for the Aged in Nineteenth-Century Philadelphia." *Pennsylvania Magazine of History and Biography* 101 (1977): 240–57.

Hershberg, Theodore. *Philadelphia: Work, Space, Family, and Group Experience in the Nineteenth Century.* New York, 1981.

Juliani, Richard N. "The Social Organization of Immigration: The Italians in Philadelphia." Ph.D. thesis, University of Pennsylvania, 1971.

Kantrow, Louise. "The Demographic History of a Colonial Aristocracy: A Philadelphia Case Study." Ph.D. thesis, University of Pennsylvania, 1976.

Klinefelter, Walter. *The ABC Books of the Pennsylvania Germans.* Publications of the Pennsylvania German Society #7. Breiningsville, Pa., 1973.

Lasch, Christopher. *Haven in a Heartless World: The Family Besieged.* New York, 1977.

Levy, Barry. "Tender Plants: Quaker Farmers and Children in the Delaware Valley, 1681–1735." *Journal of Family History* 3 (1978): 116–35.

Long, Amos, Jr. *The Pennsylvania German Family Farm.* Publications of the Pennsylvania German Society #6. Breiningsville, Pa., 1972.

Moore, John M., ed. *Friends in the Delaware Valley: Philadelphia Yearly Meeting 1681–1981.* Haverford, Pa., 1981.

Oberholtzer, Ellis P. *Literary History of Philadelphia.* Philadelphia, 1906.

Packard, Francis Randolph. *History of Medicine in the United States.* 2 vols. New York, 1932.

Palmer, Gladys Louise. *Philadelphia Workers in a Changing Economy.* Philadelphia, 1956.

Rauch, Julia B. "Quakers and the Founding of the Philadelphia Society for Organizing Charitable Relief and Repressing Mendicancy." *Pennsylvania Magazine of History and Biography* 98 (1974): 438–55.

Rosenberg, Charles. "Sexuality, Class, and Role in 19th Century America." *American Quarterly* 25 (1973): 131–54.

Saunders, John A. *100 Years After Emancipation: History of the Philadelphia Negro 1787 to 1963.* Philadelphia, 1963.

Smith-Rosenberg, Carroll. *Religion and the Rise of the American City.* Ithaca, N.Y., 1971.

Wallace, Anthony. *Rockdale.* New York, 1978.

Warner, Sam Bass. *The Private City: Philadelphia in Three Periods of Its Growth.* Philadelphia, 1968.

Wolf, Edwin, and Maxwell Whiteman. *The History of the Jews of Philadelphia from Colonial Times to the Age of Jackson.* Philadelphia, 1956.

HISTORY—WOMEN'S

Art

Brandywine River Museum. *Women Artists in the Howard Pyle Tradition.* Exhibition Catalogue. Chadds Ford, Pa., 1975.

Brodsky, Judith, and Ofelia Garcia. *Printed by Women.* Philadelphia, 1983.

Moore College of Art. *Design for Women A History of the Moore College of Art.* Wynnewood, Pa., 1968

Pennsylvania Academy of the Fine Arts. *The Pennsylvania Academy and Its Women 1850 to 1920.* Exhibition Catalogue. Philadelphia, 1974.

Rubinstein, Charlotte Streifer. *American Women Artists from Early Indian Times to the Present.* Boston, 1982.

Clubs and Associations

Croly, Jane C. *The History of the Woman's Club Movement in America.* New York, 1898.

Howe, Barbara. "Clubs, Culture and Charity: Anglo-American Upper Class Activities in the Late Nineteenth-Century City." Ph.D. thesis, Temple University, 1976.

New Century Club History, As Told at the Coming of Age Celebration: 1877–1898. Philadelphia, 1899.

Reishtein, Eleanor Fein. "Minutes of the West Grove Housekeepers Association as Source Material for Folklife Studies." *Pennsylvania Folklife* 21 (1971): 16–25.

Documentary

Beard, Mary Ritter, ed. *America Through Women's Eyes.* New York, 1933.

Cunningham, Barbara. "An Eighteenth-Century View of Femininity as Seen Through the Journals of Henry Melchior Muhlenberg." *Pennsylvania History* 43 (1976): 197–212.

Lerner, Gerda. *Black Women in White America: A Documentary History.* New York, 1972.

———. *The Female Experience: An American Documentary.* Indianapolis, 1977.

Marcus, Jacob R. *The American Jewish Woman: A Documentary History.* New York, 1981.

Women 1500–1900. Catalogue of a Joint Exhibition of the Historical Society of Pennsylvania and the Library Company of Philadelphia. Philadelphia, 1974.

Education

Conyers, Charline Fay Howard. "A History of the Cheyney State Teachers College 1837–1951." Ed.D. thesis, New York University, 1960.

Johnson, Mary. "Madame Rivardi's Seminary in the Gothic Mansion." *Pennsylvania Magazine of History and Biography* 104 (1980): 3–38.

Kerber, Linda K. "Daughters of Columbia: Educating Women for the Republic, 1787–

1805." In *The Hofstadter Aegis: A Memorial,* ed. Stanley Elkins and Eric McKitrick. New York, 1974.

McCurdy, Mary Burton Derrickson. "A Glimpse of Boarding School Education for Girls in Newark Delaware, in 1838 and 1839." *Delaware History* 17 (1976): 147–53.

Meigs, Cornelia. *What Makes a College? A History of Bryn Mawr.* New York, 1956.

Perkins, Linda Maria. "Institute for Colored Youth: A Model of 19th-Century Black Female Educational and Community Leadership 1837–1902." Ph.D. thesis, University of Illinois, Urbana-Champaign, 1978.

Sack, Saul. "The Higher Education of Women in Pennsylvania." *Pennsylvania Magazine of History and Biography* 83 (1959): 29–73.

Straub, Jean S. "Benjamin Rush's Views on Women's Education." *Pennsylvania History* 34 (1967): 147–57.

Wharton, Anne H. *Salons: Colonial and Republican Philadelphia.* Philadelphia, 1900.

Family

Brouwer, Merle G. "Marriage and Family Life Among Blacks in Colonial Pennsylvania." *Pennsylvania Magazine of History and Biography* 99 (1975): 368–72.

Degler, Carl N. *At Odds: Women and the Family in America from the Revolution to the Present.* New York, 1981.

Smith-Rosenberg, Carroll. "The Female World of Love and Ritual: Relations Between Women in the Nineteenth Century." *Signs* 1 (1975): 1–29.

Law

Endlich, Gustav A., and Louis Richards. *Rights and Liabilities of Married Women Concerning Property, Contracts, and Torts, Under the Common and Statute Law of Pennsylvania.* Philadelphia, 1889.

Goldberg, Cecile Sylvia. *Law of Married Women in Pennsylvania.* Philadelphia, 1940.

Meehan, Thomas R. " 'Not Made Out of Levity,' Evolution of Divorce in Early Pennsylvania." *Pennsylvania Magazine of History and Biography* 92 (1968): 441–64.

Nelson, William, ed. "The Early Marriage Laws of New Jersey and the Precedents on Which They Were Founded." In *Documents Relating to the Colonial History of the State of New Jersey* (Archives of the State of New Jersey) 1st Series, 22. Trenton, 1900.

Paul, Alice. *Outline of the Legal Position of Women in Pennsylvania, 1911.* Philadelphia, 1911.

Literature

Hart, John S. *The Female Prose Writers of America.* Philadelphia, 1851.

Stearns, Bertha Monica. "Philadelphia Magazines for Ladies, 1830–1860." *Pennsylvania Magazine of History and Biography* 69 (1945): 207–19.

Medicine and Science

Alsop, Gulielma F. *History of the Woman's Medical College, Pennsylvania, 1850–1950.* Philadelphia, 1950.

Blackwell, Elizabeth. *Pioneer Work for Women.* New York, 1914.

Mead, Kate Campbell. *History of Women in Medicine.* Haddam, Conn., 1938.

Nutting, Mary Adelaide, and Lavinia L. Dock. *A History of Nursing.* 4 vols. New York, 1907–12.

Smith-Rosenberg, Carroll, and Charles Rosenberg. "The Female Animal: Medical and Biological Views of Woman and Her Role in Nineteenth-Century America." *Journal of American History* 60 (1973): 332–56.

Stephenson, Mary Virginia. *First Fifty Years of the Training School for Nurses of the Hospital of the University of Pennsylvania.* Philadelphia, 1940.

Zahm, John Augustine (H.J. Mozans). *Women in Science.* New York, 1913.

Religion

Bacon, Margaret H. *As the Way Opens: The Story of Quaker Women in America.* Richmond, Ind., 1980.

——. "Quaker Women and the Charge of Separatism." *Quaker History* 69 (1980): 23–26.

Calvo, Janis. "Quaker Women Ministers in Nineteenth Century America." *Quaker History* 63 (1974): 75–93.

Dunn, Mary Maples. "Saints and Sisters: Congregational and Quaker Women in the Early Colonial Period." *American Quarterly* 30 (1978): 582–601.

Logue, Maria Kostka. *Sisters of St. Joseph of Philadelphia.* Westminster, Md., 1950.

Marcus, Jacob R. *The American Jewish Woman, 1654–1980.* New York, 1981.

Social—Miscellaneous Topics

Benson, Mary Sumner. *Women in 18th Century America: A Study of Opinion and Social Usage.* New York, 1935.

Berkin, Carol, and Mary Beth Norton. *Women of America: A History.* Boston, 1979.

Cordato, Mary Francis. "Towards a New Century: Women and the Philadelphia Centennial Exhibition, 1876." *Pennsylvania Magazine of History and Biography* 107 (1983): 113–35.

Hymowitz, Carol, and Michaele Weissman. *A History of Women in America.* New York, 1978.

Kerber, Linda K. *Women of the Republic. Intellect and Ideology in Revolutionary America.* Chapel Hill, 1980.

Lerner, Gerda. *The Woman in American History.* Reading, Mass., 1971.

Macksey, Joan, and Kenneth Macksey. *The Book of Woman's Achievements.* New York, 1976.

Melder, Keith E. *Beginnings of Sisterhood.* New York, 1977.

Norton, Mary Beth. *Liberty's Daughters: The Revolutionary Experience of American Women.* Boston, 1980.

Ryan, Mary. *Womanhood in America: From Colonial Times to the Present.* New York, 1975.

Shammas, Carole. "The Female Social Structure of Philadelphia in 1775." *Pennsylvania Magazine of History and Biography* 107 (1983): 69–83.

Smith-Rosenberg, Carroll. "The Hysterical Woman: Sex Roles and Role Conflict in 19th Century America." *Social Research* 39 (1972): 652–78.

——. "The New Woman and the New History." *Feminist Studies* 3 (1975): 185–98.

Soderlund, Jean R. "Black Women in Colonial Pennsylvania." *Pennsylvania Magazine of History and Biography* 107 (1983): 49–68.

Bell, Marion L. *Crusade in the City: Revivalism in Nineteenth-Century Philadelphia.* Lewisburg, Pa., 1977.

Bronner, Edwin. "An Early Example of Political Action by Women." *Friends Historical Association Bulletin* 43 (1954): 29–32.

Brown, Ira V. "Cradle of Feminism: The Female Anti-Slavery Society 1833–1840." *Pennsylvania Magazine of History and Biography* 102 (1978): 143–66.

———. "The Woman's Rights Movement in Pennsylvania, 1848–1873." *Pennsylvania History* 32 (1965): 153–65.

Drinker, Sophie H. "Votes for Women in 18th Century New Jersey." *New Jersey Historical Society Proceedings* 80 (1962): 31–45.

Flexner, Eleanor. *Century of Struggle: The Woman's Rights Movement in the U.S.* Rev. ed. Cambridge, Mass., 1975.

Foner, Philip S., ed. "A Pennsylvania State Senator on Women's Rights in 1868." *Pennsylvania History* 41 (1974): 423–26.

Katzenstein, Caroline. *Lifting the Curtain: The State and National Woman Suffrage Campaigns in Pennsylvania as I Saw Them.* Philadelphia, 1955.

Krone, Henrietta Louise. "Dauntless Women: The Story of the Women Suffrage Movement in Pennsylvania, 1910–1920." Ph.D. thesis, University of Pennsylvania, 1946.

Lutz, Alma. *Crusade for Freedom: Women in the Antislavery Movement.* Boston, 1968.

Mahoney, Joseph F. "Woman Suffrage and the Urban Masses." *New Jersey History* 87 (1969): 151–72.

O'Connor, Lillian. *Pioneer Women Orators; Rhetoric in the Ante-Bellum Reform Movement.* New York, 1954.

Philbrook, Mary. "Woman's Suffrage in New Jersey Prior to 1807." *New Jersey Historical Society Proceedings* 57 (1939): 87–98.

Preston, L. E. "Speakers for Women's Rights in Pennsylvania." *Western Pennsylvania Historical Magazine* 54 (1971): 245–63.

Rauch, Julia B. "Unfriendly Visitors: The Emergence of Scientific Philanthropy in Philadelphia, 1878–1880." Ph.D. thesis, Bryn Mawr College, 1974.

———. "Women in Social Work: Friendly Visitors in Philadelphia, 1880." *Social Service Review* 49 (1975): 241–59.

Smith, Thelma M. "Feminism In Philadelphia, 1790–1850." *Pennsylvania Magazine of History and Biography* 68 (1944): 243–68.

Stanton, Elizabeth Cady et al., eds. *History of Woman Suffrage.* 6 vols. New York, 1881.

Sutherland, John F. "The Origins of Philadelphia's Octavia Hill Association: Social Reform in the 'Contented' City." *Pennsylvania Magazine of History and Biography* 99 (1975): 20–44.

Watson, Frank Dekker. *The Charity Organization Movement in the U.S., A Study in American Philanthropy.* New York, 1922.

Wittenmyer, Annie. *History of the Woman's Temperance Crusade.* Boston, 1882.

Woman's Christian Temperance Union, Pennsylvania. *History of the Pennsylvania Woman's Christian Temperance Union.* Quincy, Pa., 1937.

War and Peace

Brocket, Linus P., and Mary C. Vaughan. *Woman's Work in the Civil War.* Philadelphia, 1867.

Bussey, Gertrude C., and Margaret Tims. *Women's International League for Peace and Freedom, 1915–1965.* London, 1965.
De Pauw, Linda Grant. *Fortunes of War: New Jersey Women and the American Revolution.* Trenton, 1976.

Work

Baker, Elizabeth. *Technology and Woman's Work.* New York, 1964.
Baxandall, Rosalyn, Linda Gordon, and Susan Reverby. *America's Working Women: A Documentary History—1600 to the Present.* New York, 1976.
Bennett, Helen C. *American Women in Civic Work.* New York, 1915.
Harris, Barbara J. *Beyond Her Sphere: Women and the Professions in American History.* Westport, Conn., 1978.
Hill, Joseph Adna. *Women in Gainful Occupations, 1870–1920.* Washington, D.C., 1929.
Kessler-Harris, Alice. *Women Have Always Worked.* Old Westbury, N.Y., 1982.
Klaczynska, Barbara. "Why Women Work: A Comparison of Various Groups—Philadelphia, 1910–1930." *Labor History* 17 (1976): 73–87.
―――. "Working Women in Philadelphia 1900–1930." Ph.D. thesis, Temple University, 1975.
Manges, Francis M. "Women Shopkeepers, Tavern-Keepers, and Artisans in Colonial Philadelphia." Ph.D. thesis, University of Pennsylvania, 1958.
Meyer, Annie Nathan, ed. *Woman's Work in America.* New York, 1891.
Mossell, Mrs. N. F. *Work of the Afro-American Women.* Philadelphia, 1894.
Oakley, Ann. *Woman's Work: The Housewife, Past and Present.* New York, 1974.
O'Neill, William L., comp. *Women at Work.* Alexandria, Va., 1972.
O'Sullivan, Judith, and Rosemary Gallick. *Workers and Allies: Female Participation in the American Trade Union Movement, 1824–1976.* Exhibition Catalogue, Smithsonian Institution. Washington, D.C., 1975.
Palmer, Gladys Louise. *The Industrial Experience of Women Workers at the Summer Schools, 1928 to 1930.* Bulletin of the U.S. Women's Bureau #89. Washington, D.C., 1931.
―――. *Union Tactics and Economic Change: A Case Study of Three Philadelphia Textile Unions.* Philadelphia, 1932.
Perry, Lorinda. *The Millinery Trade in Boston and Philadelphia: A Study of Women in Industry.* Binghamton, N.Y., 1916.
Pinchbeck, Ivy. *Women Workers and the Industrial Revolution.* 1750–1850. London, 1930.
Salinger, Sharon V. " 'Send No More Women': Female Servants in Eighteenth-Century Philadelphia." *Pennsylvania Magazine of History and Biography* 107 (1983): 29–48.
Stern, Madeleine B. *We the Women. Career Firsts of Nineteenth-Century America.* Reprint. New York, 1974.

STATISTICAL WORKS

Philadelphia County Medical Society, Committee on Maternal Welfare. *Maternal Mortality in Philadelphia, 1931–1933.* Philadelphia, 1934.
U. S. Women's Bureau. *The Legal Status of Women in the United States of America,*

January 1, 1948: Report for Pennsylvania. GPO Bulletin #157–37. Washington, D.C., 1949.

————. *Women in Delaware Industries: A Study in Hours, Wages, and Working Conditions.* GPO Bulletin #58. Washington, D.C., 1927.

————. *Women in New Jersey Industries: A Study of Wages and Hours.* GPO Bulletin #37. Washington, D.C., 1924.

————. *Women Office Workers in Philadelphia.* By H. A. Byrne. GPO Bulletin #96. Washington, D.C., 1932.

"The Useful and the Beautiful: or, Domestic and Moral Duties Necessary to Social Happiness," Frontispiece, 1850 (Library Company of Philadelphia)

APPENDIX

Appendix 1

A GUIDE TO THE RESOURCES FOR WOMEN'S HISTORY IN THE PHILADELPHIA AREA

Questionnaire Instructions

The overall purpose of this questionnaire is to find materials in Philadelphia area collections relating to women's history. Specifically, this covers books, manuscripts, artwork, and artifacts that illustrate the lives of women, their accomplishments, and the attitudes toward them held both by society and by women themselves. It includes works created by or about women, implements invented or used primarily by women, and materials on the professional, amateur, and domestic activities of women.

Our aim is to get as much information from a variety of organizations as possible without imposing an undue burden on institutional personnel. Therefore, the questionnaire does not require long written answers, but simply presents topics to be checked. We do ask for dates covered and size of collections. For the latter, an estimate is sufficient if you have no hard figures.

The form includes a cover sheet for general information on your institution, followed by two parts, one for books, manuscripts, etc., and one for art works, artifacts, etc. Some organizations may need to fill out one part, others may need to fill out both.

On the cover sheet, beyond the basic information identifying the institution, we have asked for two statements on your collections. The first (State General Acquisition Policy) is a broad description of the institution as a whole; the second (Describe the Most Significant Women's Material) should be as specific as possible within the space given, and should emphasize materials that are unique to your organization. Please note that we are more interested in materials that yield information than in items important simply because of scarcity. For example, a first edition of *American Woman's Home* should be included only if it is annotated or unique in some way other than its publication date.

In Part 1, covering books and manuscripts, we have attempted to provide a comprehensive, but not overlapping choice of topics. Please read through all of them first so you may choose the ones most suited to your holdings.

Since the list of topics is neither exclusive nor complete, you may want to make use of "Other." For each topic there is a number of questions regarding the relationship of the material to women, what geographical area it covers, and the type and number of items.

In Part 2, covering museum art and artifacts, the form is somewhat different, with questions asked about a series of objects or art works. In this case, we need to know their relationship to women and their geographical origin. In both sections we are interested in items used or made by or concerning women primarily, not in those that may be used by both sexes equally. For example, an egg beater should be included; a croquet set should not. However, an illustration of women playing croquet would be included, as would a rifle if it is known to have been used by a woman.

Finally, where appropriate, we are enclosing a copy of the entry for your institution in Hinding's *Women's History Sources* and would appreciate it if you would correct and update it as necessary.

Both the completed questionnaire and the corrected Hinding should be returned by July 31 to: Women's History Project, The Mayor's Commission for Women, Room 204, City Hall, Philadelphia, Pa. 19107. A stamped, self-addressed envelope is enclosed by way of encouragement.

Thank you for your help. If you have any questions, please call Trina Vaux.

A GUIDE TO THE RESOURCES FOR WOMEN'S HISTORY
IN THE PHILADELPHIA AREA

Questionnaire

Name of Institution: _____

Nature of Institution: Library _____   Archive _____   Museum _____

Other (Specify) _____

Address: _____ Telephone Number: _____

_____

Title(s) of Person(s) Most Responsible for Materials Described Below: _____

_____

Hours: _____ Admission Fee: _____

Any Restrictions in Use: _____

Published Guides to Collections: _____

_____

_____

Size of Overall Collection: _____ Percentage of Women's Material: _____

State General Acquisition Policy and Areas of Interest, Including Dates and Geographical

Concentration: _____

_____

_____

_____

_____

_____

Describe the Most Significant Women's Material Included in Your Collection: _____

_____

_____

_____

_____

_____

_____

Name, Title, and Telephone Number of Person Filling Out Form: _____

_____

RESOURCE GUIDE QUESTIONNAIRE

PART 1—Books, Periodicals, Manuscripts, Etc.

Topic	Dates	Created by Women	Concerning Women	Philadelphia	Other (Specify)	Specify Number of Items			
						Printed	Handwritten	Machine Readable	Audio Video
Art, Architecture, Decorative Arts									
Behavior (etiquette, fashion, etc.)									
Charities									
Domestic Activity									
Education									
Law (crime, rights)									
Literature (fiction, biography, etc.)									
Medicine									
Minorities & Ethnicity									

RESOURCE GUIDE QUESTIONNAIRE

PART 1—p. 2

Topic	Dates	Created by Women	Concerning Women	Philadelphia	Other (Specify)	Specify Number of Items			
						Printed	Handwritten	Machine Readable	Audio Video
Sciences									
Performing Arts									
Reform & Feminism									
Religion									
Sex (education, preference, etc.)									
Social Life (amusements, clubs)									
Statistics (economic, demographic, etc.)									
Technology									

RESOURCE GUIDE QUESTIONNAIRE

PART 1—p. 3

Topic	Dates	Created by Women	Concerning Women	Philadelphia	Other (Specify)	Specify Number of Items			
						Printed	Handwritten	Machine Readable	Audio Video
Work (business, occupations, etc.) ———									
Other (Specify) ———									

RESOURCE GUIDE QUESTIONNAIRE

PART 2—Art, Artifacts, Implements, Etc.

Type of Material	Number of Items	Dates	Made by Women	Used by Women	Concerning Women	Philadelphia	Other (Specify)
Appliances & Equipment							
Clothing & Accessories							
Drawings							
Furniture							
Household Items							
Musical Instruments							
Paintings							
Photographs							
Prints							

RESOURCE GUIDE QUESTIONNAIRE

PART 2—p. 2

Type of Material	Number of Items	Dates	Made by Women	Used by Women	Concerning Women	Philadelphia	Other (Specify)
Religious Artifacts							
Scientific Apparatus							
Sculpture							
Textiles							
Toys & Amusements							
Other (Specify)							

Appendix 2

INSTITUTIONS TO WHICH THE QUESTIONNAIRE WAS SENT, BUT WHICH ARE NOT LISTED

The records of the following organizations are housed at repositories as shown:

American Association of University Women—at the Historical Society of Pennsylvania

B'nai B'rith Women, Greater Philadelphia Council—at the Philadelphia Jewish Archives Center

International Ladies Garment Workers Union—at the Philadelphia Jewish Archives Center and the New York headquarters of the Union

Mother Bethel African Methodist Episcopal Church—at the Historical Society of Pennsylvania

New Century Guild—at the Historical Society of Pennsylvania

Violet Oakley Foundation—distributed to various local art museums

Sun Oil Company—at the Eleutherian Mills Historical Library

Women Strike for Peace—at the Swarthmore College Peace Collection

Women's International League for Peace and Freedom—at the Swarthmore College Peace Collection

YWCA—at the Temple University Libraries—Special Collections—Urban Archives Center

The following institutions have archives, but they are closed:

Bernardine Sisters of Saint Francis (Hinding 15,337)
Handmaids of the Sacred Heart of Jesus
Medical Mission Sisters
Sisters of the Holy Redeemer
Union of Polish Women in America

The following institutions indicated that they have no historical records or unique materials, or that they did not wish to be listed in the Guide:

Afro-American Historical and Cultural Museum
American Society of Women Accountants
Burlington County Library
The Carpenter's Company
Congregation Rodeph Shalom Library
Fairmount Park Art Association

Federal Reserve Bank of Philadelphia
Fireman's Hall
First African Baptist Church
The Stephen Girard Collection
Haddonfield Public Library
Hercules Inc.
Lutheran Settlement House
Mendelssohn Club of Philadelphia
Missionary Sisters of the Sacred Heart
Montgomery County-Norristown Public Library—Steinbright Local History Collection
Morris Arboretum of the University of Pennsylvania
Mount Pisgah African Methodist Episcopal Church
Newcomen Society in North America
Pennsylvania Horticultural Society
Republican Women of Pennsylvania
Rohm & Haas Company
Springside School
Villanova University
Wagner Free Institute of Science

The following institutions did not return the Questionnaire:
The Acorn Club
American Catholic Historical Society
Artists Equity Association, Inc.
Arts Council—YM-YWHA
Beaver College
Betsy Ross Flag House
Campbell Museum
The Charlotte Cushman Club
Chinese Cultural and Community Center
Church of the Crucifixion
Coalition of Labor Union Women
Committee of 1926
Congregation Mikveh Israel
Daughters of the American Revolution
Delaware Art Museum
Democratic Women of Philadelphia
Frankford Historical Society
George School
German Society of Pennsylvania
Rebecca Gratz Club
Grey Nuns of the Sacred Heart (Hinding 15,356)
Historical Society of Haddonfield
Historical Society of Montgomery County
Ile-Ife Black Humanitarian Center
Institute of Contemporary Art of the University of Pennsylvania
Inter-Church Child Care Society (Philadelphia Social Services for Children)
International Association for Personnel Women (Hinding 15,124)
Library Company of Burlington
Lower Merion Historical Society

Mount Holly Library—Burlington County Lyceum of History and Natural Sciences
National Association of University Women
New Brunswick Public Library (Hinding 10,924)
New Brunswick Theological Seminary—Archives of the Reformed Church in America (Hinding 10,925–10,927)
New Jersey Historical Commission
News Journal Company Library
Pennsylvania Federation of Women's Clubs
Pennsylvania Judicial Selection Project
Philadelphia Archdiocesan Archives (Hinding 15,152)
Philadelphia Club of Advertising Women
Philadelphia Society for the Preservation of Landmarks
Philadelphia Women's Realty Association
Pioneer Women
Princeton University Library (Hinding 11,151–11,179)
The Print Club
Saint George's United Methodist Church
Saint Thomas Episcopal Church
Sisters of Assumption
Tindley Temple United Methodist Church
Union League of Philadelphia
University of Pennsylvania Graduate School of Education
Village Improvement Association
Vineland Historical Society
Wesley African Methodist Episcopal Zion Church
The Wistar Institute
Women in Graphic Arts
Women's Traffic Club of Philadelphia
Zoar United Methodist Church
The Zoological Society of Philadelphia

*A Class in Oral History Work, Institute for Colored Youth, Annual Report, 1911
(Historical Society of Pennsylvania)*

INDEX TO INSTITUTIONS

KEY TO ABBREVIATIONS FOR INSTITUTIONS

For institutions listed in the Library of Congress Union Catalogue or Shaw and Shoemaker's *American Bibliography A Preliminary Checklist for 1801–1834* (N.Y., 1958 –) their abbreviations are used. The others have been adapted or invented using the same system.

DeDHi-A	Delaware Division of Historical and Cultural Affairs — Archives Branch
DeGE	Eleutherian Mills Historical Library
DeHi	Historical Society of Delaware
DeU-A	University of Delaware — Archives
DeU-Wm	University of Delaware — Women's Studies Program
DeWH	The Hagley Museum
DeWint-A	The Henry Francis du Pont Winterthur Museum, Inc. — Winterthur Archives
DeWint-D	The Henry Francis du Pont Winterthur Museum, Inc. — Joseph Downs Manuscript and Microfilm Collection
DeWint-L	The Henry Francis du Pont Winterthur Museum, Inc. — Library
Nj	New Jersey State Library — Bureau of Law, Archives, and Reference Services
NjBHi	Bordentown Historical Society
NjBuHi	Burlington County Historical Society
NjCHi	Camden County Historical Society
NjGbS	Glassboro State College — Savitz Library, Special Collections
NjP	Princeton University Libraries
NjPETS	Educational Testing Service
NjP-M	Princeton University — The Art Museum
NjPS	E. R. Squibb & Sons, Inc.
NjR-AL	Rutgers University — Alexander Library
NjR-DL	Rutgers University — Mabel Smith Douglass Library
NjT	Free Public Library — Trenton, New Jersey
NjTOHP	New Jersey Office of Historic Preservation
NjVHi	Vineland Historical Society
NjWGHi	Gloucester County Historical Society
PAI	Philadelphia College of Art — Library
PAsN	Neumann College
PAsOSF	Our Lady of Angels Convent
PBa	Academy of the New Church — Archives
PBeSBS	Sisters of the Blessed Sacrament for Indians and Colored People (Motherhouse)

PPHa	Hahnemann University — Archives and History of Medicine Collections
PPHC	Philadelphia Historical Commission
PPHFC	Holy Family College
PPINA	INA Archives
PPINHP	Independence National Historical Park
PPJA	Philadelphia Jewish Archives Center
PPJL	Junior League of Philadelphia, Inc.
PPL	Library Company of Philadelphia
PPLas	La Salle College Art Museum
PPLH	Lemon Hill Mansion
PPLT	Lutheran Archives Center at Philadelphia
PPMA	The Mutual Assurance Company
PPMAJ	Museum of American Jewish History
PPMCP	Medical College of Pennsylvania, Archives and Special Collections on Women in Medicine
PPMHi	Historical Society of the Eastern Pennsylvania Conference of the United Methodist Church
PPMM	Ebenezer Maxwell Mansion, Inc.
PPMo	Moore College of Art
PPMSBT	Missionary Servants of the Most Blessed Trinity
PPO	Philadelphia Orchestra Association
PPOSBM	Sisters of Saint Basil the Great, Sacred Heart Province
PPPAFA	Pennsylvania Academy of the Fine Arts
PPPC	The Philadelphia Contributionship
PPPCl	The Plastic Club — Art Club for Women
PPPCT-P	Philadelphia College of Textiles and Science — Goldie Paley Design Center
PPPCT-PL	Philadelphia College of Textiles and Science — Pastore Library
PPPE	Diocese of Pennsylvania, Protestant Episcopal Church
PPPH	Pennsylvania Hospital
PPPM	Philadelphia Museum of Art
PPPMM	Philadelphia Maritime Museum
PPPrHi	Presbyterian Historical Society
PPPT	Perelman Antique Toy Museum
PPRF	Rosenbach Museum and Library
PPRL	Robert W. Ryerss Library and Museum
PPSD	School District of Philadelphia — Pedagogical Library
PPSF	PSFS
PPSSJ	Sisters of Saint Joseph of Philadelphia
PPT-CC	Temple University Libraries — Special Collections — Contemporary Culture Collection
PPT-CT	Temple University Libraries — Special Collections — Conwellana-Templana Collection
PPT-P	Temple University Libraries — Special Collections — Paskow Science Fiction Collection
PPT-R	Temple University Libraries — Special Collections — Rare Books and Manuscripts Collection
PPT-U	Temple University Libraries — Special Collections — Urban Archives Center
PPVHM	Sisters of the Visitation of Holy Mary
PPVO	The Volunteers for the Philadelphia Orchestra

PPWG	Women for Greater Philadelphia
PPWISP	Women's Insurance Society of Philadelphia
PPWL	The War Library and Museum of the Military Order of the United States
PPWS	Willet Stained Glass Studio, Inc.
PPWW	Philadelphia Women's Coalition — Women's Way
PPWy	Wyck
PRCL	Cabrini College Library
PRosC	Rosemont College — Library
PRosC-I	Rosemont College — Institute of Studies on the Society of the Holy Child Jesus
PRosHC	Holy Child Archives — American Province
PRosI	Agnes Irwin School
PSC-Hi	Swarthmore College — Friends Historical Library
PSC-P	Swarthmore College Peace Collection
PU-A	University of Pennsylvania — Archives
PU-HSN	School of Nursing, Hospital of the University of Pennsylvania
PU-M	University of Pennsylvania — The University Museum
PU-MA	University of Pennsylvania — The University Museum — Archives
PU-V	University of Pennsylvania — Van Pelt Library
PU-VS	University of Pennsylvania — Van Pelt Library — Special Collections
PVfNHi	Valley Forge National Historical Park
PWcHi	Chester County Historical Society
PWcT	West Chester University — Francis Harvey Green Library
PWeW	Westtown School
PWRHi	Radnor Historical Society

ART, ARCHITECTURE, DECORATIVE ARTS

BEHAVIOR (ETIQUETTE, FASHION)

EDUCATION

FEMINISM AND REFORM

GENEALOGICAL RECORDS

INTERNATIONAL EXPOSITIONS

LAW (CRIME, RIGHTS)

PHOTOGRAPHS

PRINTS

RELIGIOUS ARTIFACTS

SCIENTIFIC APPARATUS

SCULPTURE

Jewish Women's Club (Library Company of Philadelphia)

INDEX TO NOTABLE DELAWARE VALLEY WOMEN

164

*Index to
Notable
Delaware
Valley
Women*

166

Index to
Notable
Delaware
Valley
Women

167

*Index to
Notable
Delaware
Valley
Women*

168

*Index to
Notable
Delaware
Valley
Women*

Penn, Hannah Callowhill, 108
Printz, Maria von Linnestau, 108

PUBLISHING

Duane, Margaret Hartman Markoe
    Bache, 101
Goddard, Mary Katherine, 103

REFORM—CIVIC

Allen, Sarah Bass, 98
Blankenburg, Lucretia Longshore, 99
Burnham, Mary Arthur, 99
Carson, Anna Lea Baker, 100
Cohen, Mary Matilda, 100
Cohen, Matilda Samuel, 100
Day, Anna Blakiston, 100
Ely, Gertrude S., 101
Fisher, Elizabeth Wilson, 102
Fleisher, Helen, 102
Freeman, Corinne Keen, 102
Gage, Frances Dana Barker, 102
Gillespie, Elizabeth Duane, 102
Hallowell, Sarah Catherine Fraley, 103
Hancock, Cornelia, 103
Harper, Frances Ellen Watkins, 103
Ingham, Mary Hall, 104
Kelley, Florence, 105
Lea, Caroline Tyler Brown, 105
Lippincott, Alice, 105
Lippincott, Joanna Wharton, 105
Lorimer, Alma Viola Ennis, 106
Luckie, Mary Barton, 106
Martin, Elizabeth Price, 106
Mumford, Mary Eno Bassett, 107
Oberholtzer, Sara Louisa, 107
Oakley, Imogen Brashear, 107
Parrish, Helen, 107
Pemberton, Caroline Hollingsworth,
    108
Shelton, Matilda Hart, 109
Simpson, Ellen Holmes Verner, 109
Smith, Hannah Whitall, 109
Stevenson, Sara Yorke, 110
Warner, Emalea Pusey, 111
Wharton, Susanna Parrish, 111
White, Caroline Earle, 111
Wister, Frances Anne, 111

Wister, Mary Channing Wister, 111
Wittenmyer, Annie Turner, 111
Worrell, Emma, 111

REFORM—LABOR

Bellanca, Dorothy Jacobs, 98
Bloor, Ella Reeve, 99
Grossman, Mary Foley, 103
Marot, Helen, 106
Miller, Frieda Segelke, 106

RELIGION

American Methodist Episcopal
    Allen, Sarah Bass, 98
    Lee, Jarena, 105
Episcopalian
    Markoe, Matilda Campbell, 106
Jewish
    Gratz, Rebecca, 103
Lutheran
    Kugler, Anna Sarah, 105
Methodist
    Shaw, Anna Howard, 109
    Wittenmyer, Annie Turner, 111
Presbyterian
    Hoge, Jane Currie Blaikie, 104
Quaker
    Bettle, Jane Temple, 99
    Branson, Julia, 99
    Bringhurst, Hannah, 99
    Brinton, Anna Shipley, 99
    Cadbury, Emma, 100
    Cresson, Sarah, 100
    Gummere, Amelia Mott, 103
    Gurney, Eliza Paul Kirkbride, 103
    Hill, Hannah Lloyd Delavall, 104
    Johnson, Emily Cooper, 104
    Jones, Rebecca, 104
    Kite, Mary, 105
    Morris, Susanna, 107
    Mott, Lucretia Coffin, 107
    Price, Rachel Kirk, 108
    Rushmore, Jane P., 109
    Smith, Hannah Whitall, 109
Roman Catholic
    Bachman, Mother Mary Francis, 98
    Banach, Sister M. Martina, 98

169

*Index to
Notable
Delaware
Valley
Women*

170

*Index to
Notable
Delaware
Valley
Women*

171

*Index to
Notable
Delaware
Valley
Women*

WAR RELIEF

WARFARE